ECONOMIC ISSUES, PROBLEMS AND PERSPECTIVES

UNEMPLOYMENT INSURANCE

ISSUES, CHALLENGES AND PERSPECTIVES

ECONOMIC ISSUES, PROBLEMS AND PERSPECTIVES

Additional books and e-books in this series can be found on Nova's website under the Series tab.

ECONOMIC ISSUES, PROBLEMS AND PERSPECTIVES

UNEMPLOYMENT INSURANCE

ISSUES, CHALLENGES AND PERSPECTIVES

ARLETTE BOLK
EDITOR

snova
New York

Library of Congress Cataloging-in-Publication Data

ISBN: 978-1-53614-937-1

Published by Nova Science Publishers, Inc. † New York

CONTENTS

PREFACE

Unemployment insurance (UI) is a federal-state system and mandatory AJC partner. UI benefits are available to workers who have involuntarily lost their jobs and have demonstrated a required level of labor force attachment. UI provides weekly cash payments to replace a portion of eligible workers' earnings, up to a statewide maximum. Eligibility and benefit levels vary by state, though most states offer up to 26 weeks of state-financed UI benefits through each state's Unemployment Compensation (UC) program. Certain economic conditions may extend the duration of UI benefits through the permanent Extended Benefit (EB) program.

Chapter 1 - The UI program, which is overseen by DOL and administered by states, paid $30 billion to about 5.7 million individuals in 2017. Under federal law, to be eligible for benefits, individuals are generally required to actively search for work, but the specific work search requirements vary by state. Yet, states found that some benefits were overpaid to UI claimants who were ineligible because they were not meeting work search requirements. GAO was asked to review improper payments due to UI claimants' failure to actively search for work. Building on GAO's prior work (GAO-18-133R), this chapter examines (1) state administrative practices associated with work search overpayments; (2) selected states' approaches to address work search overpayments; and (3) DOL's oversight and support of states' efforts.

GAO analyzed DOL data, including the results of state reviews of a representative random sample of UI payments made from fiscal years 2013 through 2017. GAO also reviewed UI information from six states selected for variation in work search requirements and overpayment rates, interviewed DOL and state officials, and reviewed relevant federal laws, regulations, and guidance.

Chapter 2 - The 115th Congress continues to consider many issues related to the two major components of the unemployment insurance (UI) system: Unemployment Compensation (UC) and Extended Benefits (EB). This chapter provides short summaries of legislative proposals with respect to UI programs. It also gives a brief overview of the UI programs that may provide benefits to eligible unemployed workers. In addition, it briefly summarizes UI proposals included in the President's budget for FY2019.

President Trump signed H.J.Res. 42 on March 30, 2017 (P.L. 115-17). This Congressional Review Act (CRA) resolution negated 20 C.F.R. Part 620. This now-negated rule had set out the circumstances under which states were allowed to prospectively drug test UC claimants based upon the prevalence of drug testing in the occupations in which they were seeking employment. Additionally, President Trump signed P.L. 115-123, the Bipartisan Budget Act of 2018, on February 9, 2018. Among other provisions, P.L. 115-123 includes two types of UI provisions: (1) codification of Reemployment Services and Eligibility Assessments (RESEAs) for UI beneficiaries, including funding and other requirements; and (2) a deferral of outstanding interest on federal UI loans for the U.S. Virgin Islands.

This chapter also describes UI legislation proposed in the 115th Congress that addresses the following:

- Rehiring UI beneficiaries and exhaustees—H.R. 3702 and H.R. 4470
- Vouchers and demonstration projects—H.R. 1091
- Additional UI benefits for certain energy workers—S. 987 and H.R. 3314
- Drug Testing—H.R. 3330

For a brief overview of UC, see CRS In Focus IF10336, *The Fundamentals of Unemployment Compensation*.

Chapter 3 - The 114th Congress considered many issues related to unemployment insurance (UI) programs: Unemployment Compensation (UC), the temporary, now-expired Emergency Unemployment Compensation (EUC08), and Extended Benefits (EB). This chapter gives a brief overview of the UI programs that may provide benefits to eligible unemployed workers. In addition, it briefly summarizes the President's budget proposal for FY2017.

The National Defense Authorization Act for Fiscal Year 2016, P.L. 114-92, altered certain conditions for individuals to receive Unemployment Compensation for Former Service members (UCX).

This chapter also describes UI legislation proposed in the 114th Congress that addressed:

- Concurrent receipt of Social Security Disability Insurance (SSDI) and UI benefits—S. 343, S. 499, H.R. 5919, H.R. 918, and S. 2005
- UI program integrity—H.R. 2503 and H.R. 2512
- Unemployment Compensation for Former Service members (UCX)—P.L. 114-92, S. 1376, and H.R. 1735
- Drug testing—H.R. 1136, H.R. 2148, and H.R. 5945
- Rehiring UI beneficiaries and exhaustees—H.R. 481, H.R. 2265, H.R. 2721, H.R. 3555, H.R. 3622, H.R. 4593, H.R. 4973 and S. 1517
- Reauthorization of EUC08—H.R. 2721 and H.R. 3555
- Vouchers and demonstration projects—H.R. 2509, H.R. 2721, and H.R. 3555
- Job training and education—H.R. 2219
- Relocation Subsidies—H.R. 2755
- Short-time Compensation (STC)—H.R. 2721, H.R. 3555, H.R. 5408, and S. 1902
- New benefits for certain energy workers—H.R. 5669 and S. 2398

- Domestic violence—H.R. 3841 and S. 2208

For a brief overview of UC, see CRS In Focus IF10336, *The Fundamentals of Unemployment Compensation*.

Chapter 4 - The federal government supports several programs that can provide assistance to workers who lose their jobs as a result of a natural or other disaster. In many cases, disaster-affected workers will be served by permanent programs and systems that generally provide assistance to workers who involuntarily lose their jobs. In some cases, disaster-triggered federal supports may be made available to provide additional assistance or aid to workers who do not qualify for assistance under the permanent programs.

This chapter discusses two income support programs and two workforce service programs. In each benefit category, there is a broader permanent program and a more-targeted program for disaster-affected workers. All of these programs are administered through state agencies and some programmatic details may be state-specific.

- Unemployment Compensation (UC) provides a weekly cash payment to workers who are involuntarily unemployed and meet other criteria. States administer UC benefits with U.S. Department of Labor (DOL) oversight. UC benefits are considered entitlements for eligible workers and funded via payroll taxes paid by employers.
- Disaster Unemployment Assistance (DUA) provides a weekly cash payment to individuals who become unemployed as a direct result of a major disaster and are not eligible for UC benefits. DUA is funded by the federal government and benefits are paid through each state's UC agency.
- Dislocated Worker Activities under the Workforce Innovation and Opportunity Act (WIOA-DW) are federal formula grants to states to provide training and career services to workers who involuntarily lose their jobs and meet other criteria. WIOA-DW

grants are funded via DOL appropriations and administered by state workforce agencies and local partners with DOL oversight.

- Disaster Dislocated Worker Grants (DDWGs) are competitive federal grants that support temporary disaster response jobs for workers who are unemployed as a direct result of a disaster. DDWGs are awarded by DOL to the state and local partners that receive WIOA-DW funds.

Since UC and DUA outlays increase as the need grows, these funds can be responsive to the scale of a disaster. Conversely, WIOA-DW and DDWG funds are limited by appropriations levels and therefore may be less immediately scalable than UC and DUA, which are entitlements for individuals.

In some instances, Congress has enacted legislation to temporarily expand these programs that serve disaster-affected workers or otherwise extend supplemental support to the states administering them. These prior efforts may serve as a model when Congress considers legislation to support workers affected by disasters.

Chapter 5 - Federal law permits states to restrict an individual's Unemployment Compensation (UC) benefit eligibility for certain circumstances related to the "fact or cause" of unemployment; this includes situations in which an individual was fired for drug use or refusing to take a drug test. Most states have specific disqualifications for drug-related job loss, including reporting to work under the influence of drugs/alcohol; violating the employer's drug policy, including refusing to undergo drug or alcohol testing; or having tested positive for drugs or alcohol under certain circumstances. Proposals to expand drug testing in the UC program have been considered in recent (113th, 114th, and 115th) Congresses. Interest in these proposals has been balanced by concerns that federal or state laws may be subject to a constitutional challenge if UC eligibility determination or ongoing receipt of UC benefits requires passing drug tests without taking into account individualized suspicion of illicit drug use.

Recent developments to expand the states' ability to drug test UC applicants and beneficiaries include the enactment of a law permitting two new types of drug testing, the issuance of guidance and regulations to support the implementation of the law, the overturning of these regulations, and the Trump Administration's announcement of intent to propose a new drug testing rule.

Chapter 6 - Although states have a great deal of autonomy in how they establish and run their unemployment insurance programs, federal law requires states to pay Unemployment Compensation (UC) benefits promptly as provided under state law. During some recessions, current taxes and reserve balances may be insufficient to cover state obligations for UC benefits. States may borrow funds from the federal loan account within the Unemployment Trust Fund (UTF) to meet UC benefit obligations.

This chapter summarizes how insolvent states may borrow funds from the UTF loan account to meet their UC benefit obligations. It includes the manner in which states must repay federal UTF loans. It also provides details on how the UTF loans may trigger potential interest accrual and explains the timetable for increased net Federal Unemployment Taxes Act (FUTA) taxes if the funds are not repaid promptly.

Chapter 7 - Many federally funded programs that assist unemployed workers are co-located and coordinated through state-run American Job Centers (AJCs; also known as One-Stop Career Centers). The specific set of benefits and services available to a worker through the AJC network varies by the worker's characteristics and reason for unemployment.

Unemployment insurance (UI) is a federal-state system and mandatory AJC partner. UI benefits are available to workers who have involuntarily lost their jobs and have demonstrated a required level of labor force attachment. UI provides weekly cash payments to replace a portion of eligible workers' earnings, up to a statewide maximum. Eligibility and benefit levels vary by state, though most states offer up to 26 weeks of state-financed UI benefits through each state's Unemployment Compensation (UC) program. Certain economic conditions may extend the duration of UI benefits through the permanent Extended Benefit (EB) program.

AJCs coordinate a number of reemployment programs that provide job search assistance and training subsidies. These programs include both broadly available programs and targeted programs. Unlike UI benefits, which are mandatory entitlements, these employment and training programs are subject to funding caps. The primary AJC partner programs can be characterized as follows:

- *Programs available to all jobseekers* do not have eligibility requirements, though they may have limited capacity. These programs provide varied job search, training, and educational services. They include adult activities supported under the Workforce Innovation and Opportunity Act of 2014 (WIOA; P.L. 113-128), which provide reemployment services and training vouchers; Employment Services (ES) under the Wagner-Peyser Act, which provide job search assistance and other non-training services to jobseekers; and adult education programs, which provide educational services at the secondary level and below.
- *Targeted programs* provide specialized services to certain populations. These services may be targeted by the circumstances of a worker's job loss or a worker's personal characteristics. Services provided through these programs can be more intensive or more readily available than those through programs with no eligibility requirements.

In addition to these primary programs, there are also several additional employment and training programs that are required AJC partners but are limited in scope and availability. The specific services offered by these additional programs vary, but tend to be targeted toward certain populations of jobseekers.

This chapter is limited to mandatory AJC partner programs under the Workforce Innovation and Opportunity Act of 2014. Some federally funded programs with employment and training components are not AJC partners. As such, the group of programs discussed in this chapter may vary from other reviews of federal workforce programs and should not be considered exhaustive.

In: Unemployment Insurance
Editor: Arlette Bolk
ISBN: 978-1-53614-937-1

Chapter 1

UNEMPLOYMENT INSURANCE: ACTIONS NEEDED TO ENSURE CONSISTENT REPORTING OF OVERPAYMENTS AND CLAIMANTS' COMPLIANCE WITH WORK SEARCH REQUIREMENTS*

United States Government Accountability Office

ABBREVIATIONS

BAM	Benefit Accuracy Measurement Program
DOL	Department of Labor
RESEA	Reemployment Services and Eligibility Assessments
UI	Unemployment Insurance

* This is an edited, reformatted and augmented version of United States Government Accountability Office; Report to the Chairman, Subcommittee on Human Resources, Committee on Ways and Means, House of Representatives, Publication No. GAO-18-486, dated August 2018.

WHY GAO DID THIS STUDY

The UI program, which is overseen by DOL and administered by states, paid $30 billion to about 5.7 million individuals in 2017. Under federal law, to be eligible for benefits, individuals are generally required to actively search for work, but the specific work search requirements vary by state. Yet, states found that some benefits were overpaid to UI claimants who were ineligible because they were not meeting work search requirements. GAO was asked to review improper payments due to UI claimants' failure to actively search for work. Building on GAO's prior work (GAO-18-133R), this chapter examines (1) state administrative practices associated with work search overpayments; (2) selected states' approaches to address work search overpayments; and (3) DOL's oversight and support of states' efforts.

GAO analyzed DOL data, including the results of state reviews of a representative random sample of UI payments made from fiscal years 2013 through 2017. GAO also reviewed UI information from six states selected for variation in work search requirements and overpayment rates, interviewed DOL and state officials, and reviewed relevant federal laws, regulations, and guidance.

WHAT GAO RECOMMENDS

GAO is making four recommendations to DOL, including that it provide states information about its determination that the use of state formal warning policies is no longer permissible and clarify its work search verification requirements. DOL agreed with GAO's recommendations and stated that it would take action to address them.

WHAT GAO FOUND

GAO's analysis of Department of Labor (DOL) data found that certain state administrative practices, such as reviewing a higher percentage of claimant-reported work search activities and frequent use of formal warnings, were associated with lower estimated work search overpayment rates for the Unemployment Insurance (UI) program. According to DOL data, 22 states were warning claimants after the first discovered occurrence of their failure to meet work search requirements (i.e., issuing formal warnings) rather than reporting that an overpayment was made, while the other states were reporting such cases as overpayments. In 2017, DOL determined that federal law does not permit states to use such policies. GAO's analysis of DOL data shows that in fiscal year 2017, estimated work search overpayments were nearly $1.4 billion (see Figure), but would have been an estimated $1.8 billion (+/-$0.2 billion) greater if states had not issued formal warnings and established overpayments. DOL officials told GAO in July 2017 that the agency would issue a letter to states informing them that federal law does not permit them to warn claimants instead of establishing an overpayment. To date, DOL has not issued the letter. Until DOL provides states with such notification, states may continue to report inconsistent information on overpayments.

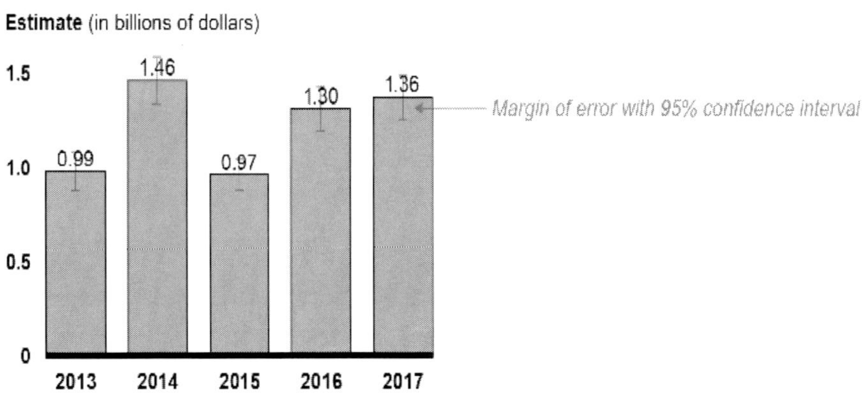

Source: GAO analysis of Department of Labor's Benefit Accuracy Measurement data. | GAO-18-486.

Estimated overpayments due to failure to meet search requirements.

State officials GAO interviewed reported using multiple approaches to address work search overpayments, including using their online systems that automate collecting information on claimants' work search activities; conducting audits of claimants work search activities beyond those required; and sending automated messages to claimants regarding their work search requirements. Officials said that their approaches encouraged claimants to conduct a more active work search and prevented work search overpayments in some cases.

DOL monitors states' work search overpayment rate estimates and has helped states address such overpayments, but lacks clear procedures for how states should verify claimants' work search activities. DOL directs states to verify a "sufficient" number of work search activities during their audits but has not provided information on what is considered sufficient. DOL data show that some states did not review claimants' work search activities for a majority of audited cases. DOL officials said that the agency plans to clarify its procedures after issuing a letter about formal warnings. By clarifying these procedures, DOL will have greater assurance that states are complying with verification requirements.

August 22, 2018

The Honorable Adrian Smith
Chairman
Subcommittee on Human Resources
Committee on Ways and Means
House of Representatives

Dear Mr. Chairman:

The federal-state Unemployment Insurance (UI) program provides temporary income support to eligible workers who become unemployed through no fault of their own. Individuals who claim unemployment are generally required to actively search for work as a condition of receiving benefits. However, the specific work search requirements—such as the number of weekly contacts a claimant must have with potential employers—vary by state, according to the Department of Labor (DOL).

Overseen by DOL, and administered by states, the UI program paid approximately $30 billion to about 5.7 million individuals in 2017. The UI program had the seventh-highest reported improper payment estimate among all federal programs in fiscal year 2017 (about $4 billion or about 12.5 percent of benefits paid).[1] Currently, the leading reported cause of UI improper payments is overpayments to claimants who failed to meet work search requirements, according to DOL data.

You asked us to review states' and DOL's approaches to address improper payments that result from UI claimants' failure to actively search for work. In November 2017, we reported that some states use formal warnings for claimants who fail to actively seek work instead of counting them as overpayments, which affects DOL's improper payment estimates, and that additional instruction from DOL could help.[2] In this chapter, we build on the findings from that prior report and provide additional information on how selected states and DOL are addressing overpayments due to claimants' failure to meet work search requirements, i.e., work search overpayments.[3]

Specifically, we examine (1) the extent to which state administrative practices are associated with reported work search overpayments, (2) the approaches that selected states have used to address work search overpayments, and (3) the extent to which DOL oversees and supports states' progress in reducing work search overpayments.

To examine the extent to which state administrative practices are associated with reported work search overpayments, we analyzed DOL's Benefit Accuracy Measurement (BAM) Program data for fiscal years 2013

---

[1] The estimate of the improper payment rate is the estimation of the following: overpayments plus underpayments as a percentage of total UI benefits paid, according to DOL documentation.

[2] GAO, *Unemployment Insurance: State Use of Warnings Related to Work Search Requirements Affects DOL's Improper Payment Estimates*, GAO-18-133R (Washington, D.C.: Nov. 21, 2017).

[3] For the purpose of this report, we refer to these overpayments as work search overpayments.

through 2017, the most recent data available.[4] We estimated work search overpayment rates and amounts overpaid, produced descriptive statistics, and conducted a regression analysis.[5] (See app. I for more information on our regression analysis.) We assessed the reliability of the data by (1) performing electronic testing of relevant data elements, (2) reviewing existing information about the data and the system that produced them, including results from prior audits, and (3) collecting information from DOL officials knowledgeable about the data. Based on these reviews, we determined that the data were sufficiently reliable for our purposes. Related to these administrative practices, we also reviewed relevant federal laws, regulations, and DOL guidance. We assessed DOL actions against its internal procedures and federal internal controls standards related to monitoring and communication.[6]

To identify approaches states have used to address work search overpayments, we reviewed documentation, such as work search verification procedures, and interviewed state UI officials from six states– Indiana, Nevada, New Jersey, Mississippi, Pennsylvania, and Utah–selected for variation in work search requirements, overpayment rates, and DOL region. Thc information we obtained from those states is not generalizable to all states.

To determine the extent to which DOL oversees and supports states' efforts to address work search overpayments, we interviewed DOL officials from the national office and collected information from all six DOL regional offices on how they oversee state BAM systems, such as monitoring procedures and state plans submitted by our selected states. We also reviewed relevant federal laws, regulations, and DOL guidance. We

---

[4] DOL's fiscal year for reporting improper payment estimates covers July 1 through June 30 of the following year. For example, DOL's fiscal year 2017 improper payment estimate covers July 1, 2016 through June 30, 2017.

[5] We developed an econometric model to analyze the relationship between states' estimated work search overpayment rates and states' administrative practices, as well as other factors captured by the BAM data that may be associated with those rates.

[6] GAO, *Standards for Internal Control in the Federal Government*, GAO-14-704G (Washington, D.C.: Sept. 10, 2014).

assessed DOL actions against its internal procedures and relevant federal internal controls standards.[7]

We conducted this performance audit from January 2017 to August 2018 in accordance with generally accepted government auditing standards. Those standards require that we plan and perform the audit to obtain sufficient, appropriate evidence to provide a reasonable basis for our findings and conclusions based on our audit objectives. We believe that the evidence obtained provides a reasonable basis for our findings and conclusions based on our audit objectives.

BACKGROUND

UI Program Administration and Funding

The federal-state UI program provides temporary cash benefits to eligible workers who lose their jobs through no fault of their own. Under this arrangement, states administer their own programs according to certain federal requirements and under the oversight of DOL's Office of Unemployment Insurance. States have considerable flexibility to set benefit amounts and their duration, or the maximum period of time that the state pays benefits, and establish eligibility requirements.

UI benefits are funded primarily through state payroll taxes on employers, and administrative costs are primarily funded through a federal payroll tax on employers. The states collect taxes that will be used to pay UI benefits, and the U.S. Department of the Treasury holds these funds in trust on behalf of the states in the Unemployment Trust Fund. DOL certifies for payment to the states administrative grants to operate their UI programs, which amounted to about $2.7 billion in fiscal year 2017. DOL is responsible for ensuring that state UI laws include certain provisions, which is a condition of the state receiving its UI administrative grant.

---

[7] GAO-14-704G.

Individuals typically claim their UI benefits by filing claims with their state UI agency online or by phone on a weekly or bi-weekly basis.[8] In fiscal year 2017, the average weekly UI benefit was about $350, and claimants remained on the program for an average of 15 weeks, according to DOL data.

Work Search Requirements for UI Claimants

Federal law establishes a work search requirement for UI eligibility, but the specific work search activities UI claimants are expected to conduct vary by state, according to a DOL report.[9] To be eligible for unemployment benefits, individuals are generally required to actively search for work under federal law.[10] The Middle Class Tax Relief and Job Creation Act of 2012 amended the Social Security Act to, among other things, require states to have work search requirements for UI claimants specified in their laws as a condition of eligibility for the states' UI administrative grants.[11] Specifically, states must have laws that require UI claimants to be "actively seeking work" as a condition of eligibility for unemployment compensation for any week. Because federal law does not specifically define actively seeking work, states have some discretion to establish a reasonable definition, according to DOL's 2013 guidance to states.[12] For example, a

---

[8] For the purposes of this report, a claimant is an individual who has applied for unemployment compensation, been found eligible, and received a first payment of benefits.

[9] Department of Labor, Employment and Training Administration, *Comparison of State Unemployment Insurance Laws* (2018).

[10] According to DOL's 2013 guidance to states, there are limited circumstances under which states may not hold claimants to the work search requirement. See DOL's Unemployment Insurance Program Letter No. 5-13. For example, according to DOL, states exempt claimants if they are participating in state-approved job training, and many states exempt claimants for other reasons depending on state law, such as if the worker is union-attached and finds work through the union hall, or if the claimant is on a temporary lay-off and there is a reasonable expectation that the worker will return to work soon. See Department of Labor, Employment and Training Administration, *Comparison of State Unemployment Insurance Laws* (2018).

[11] Pub. L. No. 112-96, § 2101, 126 Stat. 156, 159, codified at 42 U.S.C. § 503(a)(12).

[12] Department of Labor, Employment and Training Administration, Unemployment Insurance Program Letter No. 5-13, Work Search and Overpayment Offset Provisions Added to Permanent Federal Unemployment Compensation Law by Title II, Subtitle A of the Middle Class Tax Relief and Job Creation Act of 2012 (January 10, 2013).

state can specify a minimum number of weekly contacts a claimant must have with potential employers. Acceptable work search activities might also include searching for jobs online, submitting job applications, visiting a job center, attending a networking event, or establishing a LinkedIn account, according to a DOL report.[13]

Depending on the state, UI claimants may be directed to register for work with their state's Employment Service, which provides job search assistance, job placement assistance, and referrals to employers. In addition, in some cases UI claimants may be directed to participate in reemployment services at an American Job Center.[14] In 2017, DOL provided $115 million in grants to states to provide Reemployment Services and Eligibility Assessments (RESEA). RESEA services include in-person reemployment services and eligibility assessments in American Job Centers for ex-service members and UI claimants determined to have a high likelihood of exhausting their UI benefits. RESEA-funded activities include developing an individual reemployment plan, providing labor market information, identifying job skills and prospects, and reviewing the claimant's continued eligibility for UI benefits.

Process for Identifying Work Search Overpayments in State Benefit Accuracy Measurement Audits

DOL uses its Benefit Accuracy Measurement (BAM) system to determine the accuracy of UI benefit payments and estimate the amount and rate of improper payments. Under the BAM system, each state reviews a number of randomly selected cases on a weekly basis and reconstructs the UI claims process to assess the accuracy of the payments that were made.[15]

---

[13] Department of Labor, Employment and Training Administration and the National Association of State Workforce Agencies, *Re-envisioning Work Search Toolkit* (2016).

[14] American Job Centers—formerly known as one-stop centers—offer employment and training services for jobseekers in a single location.

[15] Approximately 24,000 cases are drawn from states annually, with sample sizes ranging from 360 cases per year in the 10 states with the smallest UI workloads to 480 cases in the remainder of the states.

The state determines what the benefit payment should have been according to its laws and policies. States report the results of their BAM case reviews to DOL—including overpayments and underpayments—through an online data system. DOL uses the data to estimate improper payment rates by state, as well as to calculate a nationwide rate.

State BAM audits involve reviews of existing records in the state's UI claims information system as well as original fact-finding by the state BAM investigator. DOL requires states to use a standard claimant questionnaire when conducting BAM audits. The questionnaire includes numerous questions about the claimant's circumstances—including their work search efforts—during the week under review. The questionnaire includes questions that could indicate that a claimant qualifies for an exemption from work search requirements, or made specific job contacts and the results of the job contacts, such as whether the claimant submitted an application and received a job offer.

State BAM investigators are also expected to take steps to verify the information reported by the claimant by collecting documentation from claimants and contacting employers or other third parties.[16] According to DOL's 2016 BAM annual report and BAM procedures, state BAM investigators are to review a sufficient number of work search activities to determine whether the claimant has complied with the state's minimum requirement for the number of weekly work search activities.[17] The BAM program assigns one of three classifications to each of the work search activities reviewed:

- Acceptable – Documentation exists that the work search activity reported by the claimant, such as an employer contact, employment application, or other state approved work search activity, was made

[16] Through our prior work, GAO has reported on the program integrity risks associated with relying on self-reported information to prove eligibility. See GAO, *School-Meals Programs: USDA Has Enhanced Controls, but Additional Verification Could Help Ensure Legitimate Program Access*, GAO-14-262 (Washington, D.C.: May 15, 2014).

[17] DOL, Employment and Training Administration, *IPIA 2016 Benefit Accuracy Measurement Annual Report* (Washington, D.C.: April 2017).

by the claimant and was acceptable according to the state's law or policy.

- Unverifiable – The investigator was unable to establish sufficient information to make a judgment of whether the work search activity was either acceptable or unacceptable according to the state's law or policy.[18]
- Unacceptable – Written documentation exists that the work search activity reported by the claimant was not made at all by claimant, or was made but was unacceptable according to the state's law or policy.

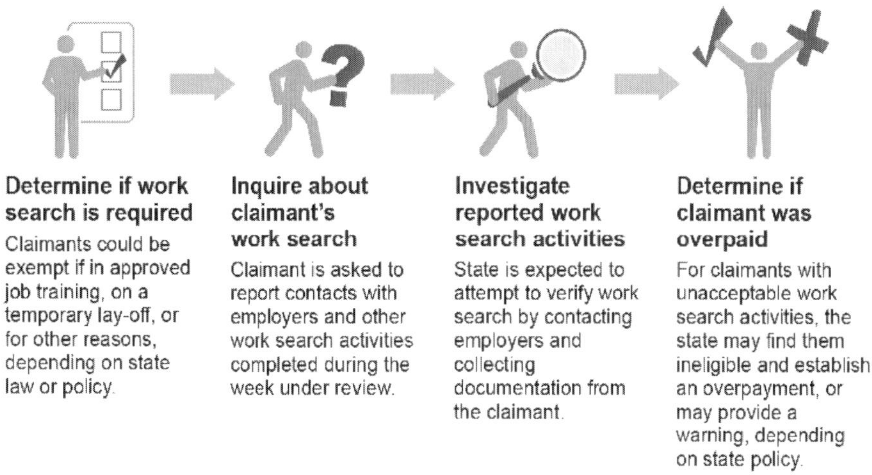

Source: GAO review of Department of Labor's Benefit Accuracy Measurement (BAM) procedures. | GAO-18-486.

Figure 1. Process for Determining if Unemployment Insurance Claimants Met Work Search Requirements in State BAM Audits.

According to DOL's BAM annual report, work search activities classified as acceptable or unverifiable may be considered in calculating whether the claimant has satisfied the state's required number of work search

[18] Through our prior work, GAO found that agencies vary in the treatment of insufficient documentation, both in identifying and in reporting the root causes of improper payments. See GAO, *Improper Payments: Actions and Guidance Could Help Address Issues and Inconsistencies in Estimation Processes*, GAO-18-377 (Washington, D.C.: May 31, 2018).

activities for purposes of BAM. If the state investigator finds that the claimant's work search is unacceptable and does not meet the state's requirements, he or she may determine the claimant was ineligible for benefits and establish an overpayment, depending on state law (see Figure 1). Currently, several states have formal warning policies and provide claimants warnings for the first instance of noncompliance with work search requirements, whereas states without these policies count these cases as overpayments, according to DOL.[19]

Reported Causes of UI Improper Payments

Since 2002, federal agencies have been required to identify and report improper payments.[20] The leading reported cause of UI improper payments in fiscal year 2017 was overpayments to claimants who failed to meet work search requirements. DOL data show that states made an estimated $1.36 billion in overpayments to such claimants in fiscal year 2017. Other major reported causes of UI improper payments in fiscal year 2017 included payments made to individuals who continue to make claims even after returning to work (benefit year earnings) and payments made to claimants who were determined ineligible due to disqualifying job separations, such

---

[19] According to DOL, states' formal warning policies vary, and there also can be variation in how they record formal warnings in the BAM program.

[20] See the Improper Payments Information Act of 2002 (IPIA), Pub. L. No. 107-300, 116 Stat. 2350, as amended by the Improper Payments Elimination and Recovery Act of 2010 (IPERA), Pub. L. No. 111-204, 124 Stat. 2224, and the Improper Payments Elimination and Recovery Improvement Act of 2012 (IPERIA), Pub. L. No. 112-248, 126 Stat. 2390 (hereinafter referred to as IPIA), codified as amended at 31 U.S.C. § 3321 note. DOL estimates and reports the improper payments for the UI program required by IPIA using the BAM system data. An improper payment is defined as any payment that should not have been made or that was made in an incorrect amount (including overpayments and underpayments) under statutory, contractual, administrative, or other legally applicable requirements. It includes any payment to an ineligible recipient, any payment for an ineligible good or service, any duplicate payment, any payment for a good or service not received (except for such payments where authorized by law), and any payment that does not account for credit for applicable discounts. See 31 U.S.C. § 3321 note. Office of Management and Budget (OMB) guidance also instructs agencies to report as improper payments any payment for which insufficient or no documentation was found.

as quitting a job without good cause or being discharged for misconduct (separation issues). (See Figure 2. Table 8 in app. II provides greater detail).

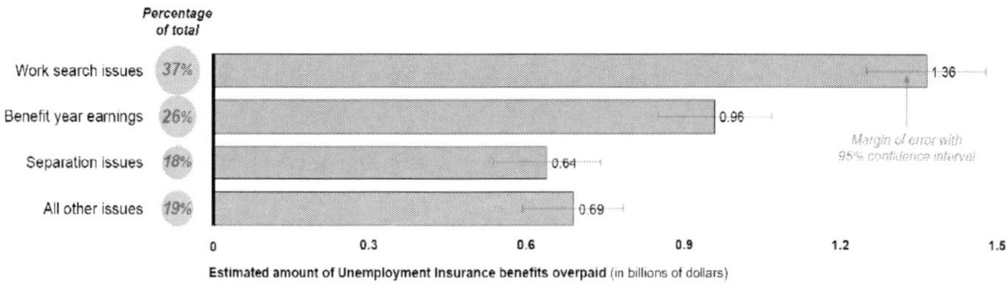

Source: GAO analysis of Department of Labor reports and Benefit Accuracy Measurement data. | GAO-18-486.

Note: Work search issues are overpayments due to claimants' failure to meet state work search requirements. Benefit year earnings are overpayments made to individuals who continued to make claims even after returning to work. Separation issues are overpayments to claimants found ineligible due to disqualifying job separations, such as quitting a job or being discharged for misconduct. All other issues include incorrect reporting of wages used to calculate benefits, able and available to work issues, employment service registration issues, and other issues.

Figure 2. Estimated Amount of Unemployment Insurance Overpayments by Cause, Fiscal Year 2017.

According to DOL officials, many UI improper payments cannot be prevented given certain legal requirements that states pay claims in a timely manner and provide claimants with due process when the state finds an eligibility issue. Specifically, according to DOL, federal law requires that when an eligibility issue is detected, the claimant has a right to receive notice and provide the state information before being denied benefits.[21] In addition, if an eligibility issue associated with work search, or any other matter, is detected but not resolved, the state is still required to pay for a claimed week no later than the week after an eligibility issue is detected, according to DOL.

---

[21] For more information, see DOL, Employment and Training Administration, Unemployment Insurance Program Letter No. 04-01, *Payment of Compensation and Timeliness of Determinations during a Continued Claims Series* (October 27, 2000) and Unemployment Insurance Program Letter No.1145, *Procedures for Implementation of the Java Decision* (November 12, 1971).

The time it takes to work through the necessary due process steps can prevent states from stopping the payment before it must be paid.

Trend in Reported Work Search Overpayments

Nationally, the estimated work search overpayment rate and the estimated amount of work search overpayments have risen in recent years. Specifically, in fiscal year 2013, approximately $1 billion in estimated work search overpayments were made to claimants who were not actively searching for work and, in fiscal year 2017, the amount increased to close to an estimated $1.36 billion (see Figure 3). The national work search overpayment rate for such claimants also increased during this time. (See Table 9 in app. II for additional details.) According to DOL officials, some states implemented more stringent work search requirements, which may account for the recent trend. As work search requirements become more stringent, the opportunities for noncompliance and errors increase and thus higher improper payment rates, according to DOL officials. While the national work search overpayment rate was 4.5 percent in fiscal year 2017, state work search overpayment rates varied widely from an estimated 0 to 41 percent of the UI benefits that states paid in fiscal year 2017.[22] (See Table 10 in app. II for state-by-state estimates of work search overpayment rates and amounts).

States use various methods to recover overpayments to UI claimants, including setting up payment plans, off-setting UI benefits, or deducting refunds from federal or state income tax returns. Like all recovered UI overpayments, recoveries of work search overpayments must be deposited in the unemployment trust fund of the state that recovered the money and can be used only for the payment of UI benefits, according to DOL officials.

[22] Seven states reported zero or close to zero work search overpayments for their sample of BAM cases in fiscal year 2017. The margin of error associated with the 95 percent confidence interval for the estimated 0 percent work search overpayment rates ranged from +/-0.7 to +/-0.8 percent. The margin of error associated with the 95 percent confidence interval for the state with a 41 percent work search overpayment rate was +/- 4.9 percent.

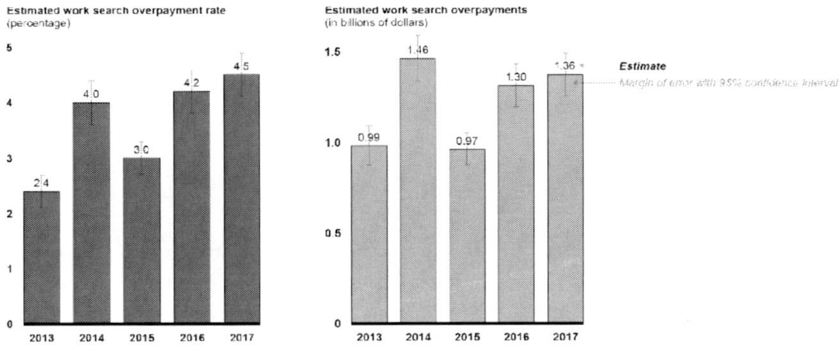

Source: GAO analysis of Department of Labor reports and Benefit Accuracy Measurement data. | GAO-18-486.

Figure 3. Estimated Rate and Amount of Unemployment Benefits Overpaid to Claimants Not Actively Searching for Work, Fiscal Years 2013-2017.

National data are not available on the amount of work search overpayments that states have recovered because, although DOL collects recovery data from states, it does not require states to separate out work search overpayment recoveries from other types of recoveries in their reporting.

Conducting More Work Search Investigations Is Associated with Lower Estimated Work Search Overpayment Rates, as Is the Use of Formal Warnings

Based on our analysis of DOL data, we found that certain state administrative practices, including investigating a higher percentage of claimant-reported work search activities and frequent use of formal warnings, were associated with lower reported state work search overpayment rates. However, DOL recently determined that federal law does not permit states to warn claimants the first time they failed to meet work search requirements (i.e., issue formal warnings) instead of establishing that an overpayment was made. Additionally, a higher percentage of claimants required to search for work is associated with higher reported state work search overpayment rates.[23]

Investigating Claimant-Reported Job Contacts Is Associated with Lower Work Search Overpayment Estimates, but the Extent to Which States Verified Contacts Varied

One of the administrative practices significantly associated with lower work search overpayment estimates was investigations of claimants' reported job contacts. Specifically, a higher percentage of cases with claimants whose contacts were investigated by the state UI agency as part of the state's BAM audit was associated with a lower work search overpayment rate estimate. According to our analysis, for every 1 percentage point increase in the percentage of cases with claimants' whose job contacts were investigated, there was a 0.072 percentage point decrease in the work search overpayment rate estimate.

The extent to which states attempted to verify claimants' reported job contacts through these investigations varied, according to our analysis of DOL data. Nationally, in fiscal year 2017, states investigated job contacts in about 80 percent of BAM cases where claimants were required to search for work. However, among the states, the proportion of cases in which job contacts were investigated was less than 50 percent in 5 states.[24] (Table 11 in app. II shows the percentage of contacts that were investigated for each state).

Furthermore, states often were not able to verify the information claimants reported. Of the job contacts that were investigated, states reported that about 48 percent of the job contacts were acceptable, about 8 percent

[23] BAM data do not include variables measuring other state practices that may be associated with work search overpayment rates, such as the number and type of employer contacts claimants are required to make and the frequency and method with which claimants report their work search activities to the state.

[24] The five states are Arkansas, Nevada, New Jersey, New York, and Pennsylvania.

were unacceptable, and about 45 percent could not be verified (see Figure 5).

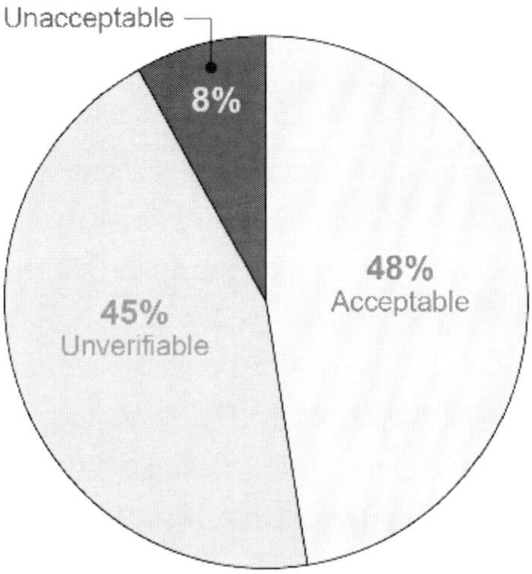

Source: GAO analysis of Department of Labor's (DOL) Benefit Accuracy Measurement (BAM) data. | GAO-18-486.

Note: Numbers do not add to 100 percent due to rounding.

Categories in the figure are defined by DOL's BAM procedures as follows:

Acceptable – work search activities are verifiable and meet states' work search requirements.

Unacceptable – work search activities reported were not conducted or did not meet state' work search requirements.

Unverifiable – state investigators could not determine whether work search activities were acceptable or unacceptable.

Figure 4. Outcomes of State Investigations of Claimant-Reported Job Contacts, Fiscal Year 2017.

Our analysis of BAM data for fiscal year 2017 also shows that for the overpayments that states were able to detect, that a large portion were found through investigating and verifying claimants' work search contacts. Specifically, 47 percent of reported work search overpayments were found through this practice. Interviewing claimants about their work search was the next most common way states detected work search overpayments.

States reported identifying 32 percent of work search overpayments in fiscal year 2017 using this practice.

Although overpayments can be the result of actions taken by the claimant or the agency administering the program, states reported that most work search overpayments are associated with claimants. For example, claimants may provide inadequate or incorrect information needed by the UI agency to determine if the claimant met work search requirements. In fiscal year 2017, states attributed about 99 percent of overpayments at least partially to claimant action, while they attributed about 2 percent at least partially to administrative errors at the state agency.[25]

Frequent Use of Formal Warnings Is Associated with Reporting Lower Work Search Overpayments, but DOL Recently Determined Their Use Is Legally Impermissible

According to DOL data, 22 states issued formal warnings to one or more claimants at some point between fiscal year 2013 and fiscal year 2017 for failure to meet work search requirements instead of finding that the claimants were overpaid. Although the states that made use of these warnings varied over this period, the number of states issuing formal warnings has generally increased over time from 13 states issuing formal warnings in fiscal year 2013 to 19 states in fiscal year 2017.[26] Overall, states that most frequently issued formal warnings had lower reported work search overpayment rates than states that did not issue formal warnings. However, their work search overpayment rates are lower because, under their state policies, they did not count an overpayment when they issued a formal warning.

---

[25] The state BAM auditor can assign responsibility for the payment error to more than one party. State administrative errors include instances of providing incorrect instructions to claimants or identifying and resolving an overpayment outside of the BAM audit process while a BAM investigation was ongoing.

[26] Although 22 states made use of formal warning s between fiscal years 2013 and 2017, not all of them consistently made use of the warnings across this period. As a result, although the number of states that used formal warnings increased over time, the states which were using this administrative practice varied in any given year.

Table 1. Average State Work Search Overpayment Rate Estimates Excluding and Including Formal Warnings by State Formal Warning Use, Fiscal Year 2017

Extent of state issuance of formal warnings	Work search overpayment rate estimates, excluding formal warnings		Work search overpayment rate estimates, including formal warnings	
	Average	Margin of error (+/-)	Average	Margin of error (+/-)
Frequent	1.4	.3	19.9	1.1
Moderate	7.9	1.3	14.1	1.8
Low	4.9	1.4	5.2	1.4
None	5.5	.4	5.5	.4

Source: GAO analysis of Department of Labor's Benefit Accuracy Measurement data. | GAO-18-486.

Note: States frequently using formal warnings are states that issued formal warnings to 75 percent or more of cases with work search errors and include 13 states. States moderately using formal warnings are states that issued formal warnings to 25 to 74.9 percent of cases with work search errors and include 4 states. States that are low users of formal warnings are states that issued formal warnings to 0.1 to 24.9 percent of cases with work search errors and include 2 states. Finally, 33 states did not use formal warnings in fiscal year 2017. Estimated work search overpayment rates represent the percentage of Unemployment Insurance benefits paid. The margin of error is associated with a 95 percent confidence interval.

Our analysis indicates that states which issued formal warnings frequently—in 75 percent or more of cases involving work search errors—had estimated work search overpayment rates that were 3.5 percentage points lower, on average, than states that did not issue formal warnings. However, states that use formal warnings less frequently—in fewer than 75 percent of cases involving work search errors—reported work search overpayment rates that were between 3 and 4 percentage points higher than states that did not issue formal warnings. See appendix I for a detailed discussion of our econometric analysis.

Table 1 shows the average work search overpayment rate estimates for each of these groups of states when formal warnings are not counted as overpayments, and the potential average work search overpayment rate when formal warnings are counted as overpayments. Excluding formal warnings, two of the groups—frequent and low users of formal warnings—had average work search overpayment rate estimates lower than the average for states that did not use formal warnings. However, when formal warnings are included in the overpayment rate, only low users of formal warnings have a work search overpayment rate estimate lower than the average for states that did not use formal warnings.

GAO's analysis of DOL data shows that in fiscal year 2017, estimated work search overpayments were nearly $1.4 billion, but potentially would have been an estimated $1.8 billion greater if states had not issued formal warnings and established overpayments. Our analysis further shows that if formal warning cases had been included in DOL's calculation of the UI overpayment rates for fiscal year 2017, the nationwide UI overpayment rate would have increased by about 6 percentage points, from an estimated 12 percent to an estimated 18 percent. Moreover, these figures represent an increase from the fiscal year 2016 figures we presented in our previous report on states' use of formal warnings related to work search requirements.[27] At that time, we found the nationwide UI overpayment rate would have increased by about 5 percentage points from an estimated 11 percent to an estimated 16 percent with the inclusion of formal warning cases. The amount of UI payments made to claimants for weeks in which they received formal warnings in fiscal year 2016 was about $1.6 billion. Table 12 in appendix II shows how the estimated UI overpayment rate in each state issuing formal warnings in fiscal year 2017 may have increased if formal warnings were not used.

State use of formal warnings has resulted in inconsistent reporting of work search overpayments, which affects DOL's reported improper payment rate for the UI program. Specifically, states that issue formal warnings have not counted as overpayments cases in which claimants did not actively search for work and received a UI benefit payment. On the other hand, states that did not have formal warning policies counted such cases as overpayments, which are factored into DOL's reported improper payments rate. The variation among states related to formal warning policies makes it difficult for DOL and others to understand the reasons behind states' reported work search overpayments.

---

[27] See GAO-18-133R.

DOL has determined and documented in its FY 2017 Agency Financial Report that the use of formal warnings is no longer allowed under the 2012 federal law, which generally requires UI claimants to actively seek work. DOL officials told us in July 2017 they would soon issue a letter to states to inform them that they are no longer permitted to use formal warnings when they determine that claimants failed to meet work search requirements. To date, DOL has not issued such a letter. In May 2018, DOL officials told us that they expect to issue the letter by the end of calendar year 2018. Federal internal control standards direct agency management to remediate identified internal control deficiencies on a timely basis. Federal internal controls standards also state that management should externally communicate the necessary quality information to achieve the entity's objectives. Additionally, these standards state that agency management should establish and operate monitoring activities to monitor the internal control system and evaluate the results.[28]

According to DOL officials, they began discussing the need for a potential discontinuation of formal warnings at conferences with states in the first half of 2017. However, we found that states continued to implement their formal warning policies, potentially resulting in an increase in the estimated amounts of overpayment dollars associated with formal warnings between fiscal year 2016 and 2017. Until DOL informs states of the need to discontinue the use of formal warnings through a letter or another mechanism, states will continue to be inconsistent in whether they count as overpayments cases in which claimants who failed to search for work in any week were provided benefits. Additionally, once DOL provides additional information to states on formal warnings, it should monitor states' responses to help ensure that DOL achieves its desired results. Furthermore, having more consistent information on overpayments related to work search issues could help DOL assess how the program is working nationwide and whether further federal and state actions would be needed to address this leading source of reported improper payments in the UI program.

---

[28] GAO-14-704G.

DOL officials stated that the national work search overpayment rate is likely to increase in the future as states begin to eliminate their formal warning practices. Officials also stated that this may take some time as some states may need to amend laws or regulations in order to do so.

Higher Percentages of Claimants Required to Search for Work Are Associated with Higher Work Search Overpayment Rate Estimates

State work search overpayment rate estimates were higher for states where a higher proportion of claimants were required to search for work. Based on our analysis, for every one percentage point increase in the fraction of cases with claimants required to search for work, there was a 0.084 percentage point increase in the work search overpayment rate estimate on average, all else being equal.

Nationwide in fiscal year 2017, states reported that work searches have been required in 80 percent of cases, with requirements in individual states ranging from 38 to 100 percent of cases. Three states reported requiring fewer than 50 percent of claimants to perform work searches, while five states reported requiring more than 95 percent of their claimants to perform work searches. The most common reasons states exempted claimants from work searches were because claimants were “job-attached” (e.g., temporarily laid-off, recalled), or they had union deferrals because they were seeking employment through their union, according to DOL data. The map in figure 6 shows the range among all the states in the percentage of UI claimants required to search for work, according to our analysis of DOL data for fiscal year 2017.[29]

[29] Table 11 in appendix II shows the percentage of claimants required to search for work in each state in fiscal year 2017.

Source: GAO analysis of Department of Labor reports and Benefit Accuracy Measurement data; U.S. Geological Survey (base map). | GAO-18-486.

Figure 5. Percentage of UI Claimants Required to Search for Work in Each State, Fiscal Year 2017.

SELECTED STATES USED MULTIPLE APPROACHES TO ADDRESS WORK SEARCH OVERPAYMENTS, BUT CITED CHALLENGES VERIFYING CLAIMANTS' WORK SEARCH ACTIVITIES

Selected states used multiple approaches to address work search overpayments, including online systems to facilitate the work search reporting and verification process, work search audits beyond the BAM audits, and messaging to inform claimants of their work search responsibilities. For example, three of six states in our review had online systems where claimants could report specific work search activities as part of filing their weekly claims, according to state officials (see Table 2).[30] Some of the approaches states used were specifically designed for UI claimants participating in state reemployment programs.

[30] Officials from the states we reviewed also reported varying work search requirements for UI claimants. See appendix III for a summary of the work search requirements for the six states included in our review.

Table 2. Approaches Used by Six Selected States to Address Work Search Overpayments

Approach	Description	States that reported using this approach
Online collection of work search information through online claims system	Online system that allows claimants to report specific work search activities when filing their weekly Unemployment Insurance claims.	Mississippi Nevada Utah
Online job search and training system	Online system that claimants can use to conduct work search activities and complete job search training.	Indiana Mississippi New Jersey Pennsylvania Utah
Work search audits	State agency randomly selects cases and attempts to verify the claimant's work search (separate from the Benefit Accuracy Measurement program).	Mississippi Pennsylvania Utah
Messaging	States provide information to claimants in different formats, such as video, print, online, or on automated phone systems, to improve claimants' understanding of work search requirements and to encourage claimants to accurately report information during the claim submission process.	Indiana Mississippi Nevada New Jersey Pennsylvania Utah

Source: GAO review of information provided by state officials and confirmed by state officials. | GAO-18-486.

State officials cited several benefits of the approaches they use to address work search overpayments. The online systems, work search audits, and messaging helped prompt work search activities and prevent work search overpayments in some cases, according to state officials. According to officials from the selected states that used them and a study on work search improper payments, online systems can facilitate the work search reporting and verification in several ways:

- **Automatically documenting the claimants' work search activities.** Online reporting of work search activities can help prevent overpayments because their work search is documented in the online claims system, which means the claimant does not need to keep a work search log.[31] In addition, online job search/training systems can be used to track the work search activities completed by claimants, making it easier for the state to verify that the work search was completed. For example, officials in Mississippi and Indiana told us they piloted an online system called NextJob and required RESEA program participants to conduct work search activities through the system. Mississippi officials reported that NextJob motivated claimants to conduct their job search and increased the speed of reemployment among these individuals. Similarly, New Jersey officials told us that UI claimants selected to participate in New Jersey's RESEA program are required to use an online job search and training system called OnRamp, which, for example, allows job seekers to create or upload their resume on the website, search for jobs, access online training, and receive email alerts on potential job matches. In addition, officials in Nevada said that the online reporting system is beneficial because the work search activities are documented in the system and are more reliably retrieved if the claimant is selected for a BAM audit because few claimants maintain and retain their work search effort logs.
- **Performing automated checks on data the claimants submit.** The online claims systems can identify potentially duplicate job contacts and check whether the claimant reported the required number of job contacts. For example, Utah officials reported that if a claimant enters job contacts from another week, officials would follow up with the claimant by phone after it is flagged by their online system. If claimants report self-disqualifying information,

[31] Nathan Wozny, Andrea Mraz Esposito, Andrew Clarkwest, Chelsea Swete, and JiHyeun Kwon-Min. "*Recommendations to OUI in Support of Efforts to Reduce Work Search Improper Payments.*" Mathematica Policy Research (Washington, D.C,: February 2012).

such as an insufficient number of job contacts, the system can automatically put a hold on a claim until the issue is resolved.

- **Facilitating communication with the claimant.** Some states added messages to their online claims system that pop up if the claimant enters incorrect or insufficient information. For example, Mississippi officials stated that they used messaging to better inform claimants of their responsibilities and to encourage them to report accurate information. According to the officials, if claimants do not report the required number of work search activities in the online system, a questionnaire will pop up requesting that the claimants explain why they did not do so. The system requires the claimants to enter more information in order to submit their claims and to receive their benefit payments. Mississippi officials also stated that adding targeted messaging resulted in fewer denials of benefits due to claimant failure to meet work search requirements and also reduced the number of appeals related to this type of denial. Some state officials said that messaging encouraged accurate reporting. For example, Indiana officials told us that at the end of the online claim filing process, claimants receive a message notifying them of the state's work search requirements and informing them that they are required to search for work to continue receiving benefits. In Utah, officials developed a video that covers claimants' responsibilities, including work search requirements, which claimants must view before receiving their initial benefit payment, according to state officials.

Officials in three of the states we reviewed reported using additional work search audits beyond BAM to help reinforce their state policies. Pennsylvania officials reported conducting 7,182 work search audits for RESEA program participants in 2016. As a result, officials reported that the state issued 1,300 warnings to claimants. The two other states— Mississippi and Utah—report that their random work search audits, coupled with their online systems, helped prevent work search overpayments as they are able to disqualify claims before the payment goes out. Mississippi and Utah officials also reported that they were also able to identify and recover some work search overpayments (see Table 3).

Despite implementing these approaches, state officials in five of the six states we contacted told us they face challenges with verifying work search activities. These officials stated that they have difficulty verifying work search activities as some claimants do not understand the work search requirements or do not keep accurate records of their work search activities, which makes it difficult for the state to confirm compliance with the state requirements. In addition, state officials also said that many employers do not keep records of job seekers' inquiries or do not respond to state requests for information when they are trying to verify claimants' work search activities. For example, Nevada officials said that work search contacts are often virtually unverifiable as many companies outsource their hiring processes to contractors who refer the job candidate for a job posting and keep the job application. Officials said these contractors also rarely respond to state inquiries about claimants' job applications. As discussed later, DOL has provided states tools to help address this issue, such as a messaging toolkit to help states improve communications with claimants and employers.

Table 3. Results of Selected State Efforts to Identify and Recover Work Search Overpayments in 2016

State	Number of claim denials due to work search non-compliance	Number of work search overpayments identified	Amount of work search overpayments	Recoveries of work search overpayments
Mississippi	22,858	2,110	$413,706	$339,045
Utah[a]	7,450	400	$146,298	$41,072

Source: GAO review of information provided by state officials. | GAO-18-486.

[a] The numbers are for the reporting year covering July 1, 2015 to June 30, 2016.

DOL Monitors States' Work Search Overpayment Rate Estimates and Provides Assistance, but Lacks Clear Procedures on Work Search Verification

DOL Monitors States' Work Search Overpayment Rate Estimates and Has Identified Strategies and Provided Tools to Help States Reduce Their Rates

DOL uses UI performance data to monitor state progress in reducing the estimated improper payment rate, including data on overpayments to claimants who failed to meet work search requirements. To do so, DOL requires states to submit State Quality Service Plans, which serve as the performance reporting and grant application documents through which states receive administrative funding. The plans include a summary of state performance on various measures related to operating the UI program, including the improper payment rate, according to DOL documentation we reviewed. States with estimated improper payment rates of 10 percent or more are required to submit corrective action plans to DOL. For example, data from two of the six states we reviewed– Nevada and New Jersey–had estimated improper payment rates above 10 percent during DOL's most recent planning cycle and developed corrective action plans. Nevada's corrective action plan noted that the state expects their rate to decline due to their June 2017 implementation of online work search reporting as part of their UI claims system. New Jersey's corrective action plan noted that the state plans to implement new online tools that will help them verify wage and employment information. DOL separately monitors each state's estimated work search overpayment rate. In addition, all states, including those who estimated improper payment rates of less than 10 percent, are required to prepare a state-specific action plan that describes the root causes of improper payments and the state's strategies to address them.[32] According to agency officials, DOL reviews plans to monitor state performance and help states identify strategies to improve performance.

Although DOL requires states with estimated improper payment rates of 10 percent or more to develop corrective action plans, according to DOL, the agency has limited options to require state UI agencies to take actions to respond to high improper payment rates. DOL officials told us that, beyond routine monitoring and providing states with technical assistance to help reduce their improper payments rate, their enforcement options are limited to withholding the state's administrative funding or removing federal tax credit reductions, which is, in effect, a tax increase for the state's employers. According to DOL officials, both are considered extraordinary sanctions that require significant due process. The agency has not withheld state administrative funding to address improper payments, according to DOL officials. DOL officials also told us that they are concerned about the effects on UI claimants if they were to withhold administrative funding. The administration's fiscal year 2019 congressional budget justification includes a legislative proposal that would authorize the Secretary of Labor to require states to implement corrective action measures for poor state performance in the UI program, helping to reduce improper payments in states with the highest estimated rates.

DOL has identified strategies to address the leading causes of UI improper payments—including work search issues—and provided states tools and funding to help implement them. For example:

- **Pathway to Reemployment Framework.** In 2016, DOL and the National Association of State Workforce Agencies published a framework that contained a broad menu of work search options that states could adopt to better reflect how individuals search for work,

[32] DOL identifies states as "high priority" and in need of more intensive technical assistance after reviewing state performance data, including the estimated improper payment rate. High priority states receive an on-site review by a team of experts, and DOL works with the states to identify strategies and action steps to improve performance. States are subject to increased DOL monitoring and technical assistance until they implement the corrective actions identified in the on-site review and sustain performance for at least six consecutive months.

such as allowing use of online job search tools to count as an approved work search activity.[33] The framework also includes suggestions for how states could document or verify claimants' work search activities for eligibility purposes.

- **Messaging toolkit.** In 2012, DOL published a messaging toolkit designed in part to improve claimants' understanding of work search requirements as a condition of eligibility for benefits.[34] According to DOL, claimants who fully understand their responsibilities and the consequences of not fulfilling them may be more likely to complete the required work search activities, thereby reducing instances of claimants' failing to search for work. DOL provided states supplemental funding to support improved messaging and tracked state implementation of the strategies.
- **Online tool to record work search activities.** In 2011, DOL provided supplemental funding to New York to develop an online work search record that could be replicated by other states. This tool is designed to reduce improper payments that result from inadequate documentation of work search activities. Claimants can use the tool to record their work search online when they file their UI claims. The work search record is automatically shared with state job centers, which in turn act to enhance claimants' work search and connect claimants with jobs. New York used open source technologies when designing the tool in an effort to help more states replicate the product at a lower cost.
- **UI Integrity Center.** The DOL-funded UI Integrity Center of Excellence (UI Integrity Center) was established as a way to help states develop and share innovative strategies to prevent and detect UI improper payments, reduce fraud, and improve program integrity.[35] For example, the UI Integrity Center funded a pilot project in 2016 to support a state in implementing an online tool that

---

[33] Department of Labor, Employment and Training Administration and the National Association of State Workforce Agencies, *Pathway to Reemployment Framework* (2016).

[34] Department of Labor, Employment and Training Administration, *UI Claimant and Employer Message Toolkit* (Washington, D.C.: Jan. 5, 2012).

[35] The UI Integrity Center is operated by the National Association of State Workforce Agencies.

trains claimants on how to effectively search for jobs and allows claimants to use the tool to complete their work search activities. The UI Integrity Center also hosted national conferences in 2016 and 2018 that included presentations on state practices to address work search improper payments.

DOL Directs States to Investigate a Sample of Claimants' Work Searches, but Has Not Clarified Procedures on Verifying Work Search

Although DOL monitors states' work search overpayment rate estimates and has provided assistance to help states address such overpayments, it has provided limited direction to states on the level of effort states must make to verify whether claimants are actively searching for work. Specifically, DOL's BAM procedures direct states to investigate a sufficient number of work search contacts in its BAM sample of UI cases to determine if the claimants met the state's work search requirement.[36] However, DOL has not provided states any additional direction on what is considered "sufficient." As previously mentioned, the extent to which states attempted to verify job contacts from claimants' work searches varied across states.[37] Some states reported to DOL that they did not investigate work search activities for a majority of their BAM cases even though work search was required and the claimant reported job contacts.

Federal internal control standards state that agency management should externally communicate the necessary quality information to achieve its objectives, including addressing related risks.[38] According to DOL officials, the agency plans to clarify its BAM procedures, to include providing more

---

[36] U.S. Department of Labor, Employment and Training Administration, *Benefit Accuracy Measurement State Operations Handbook, ET Handbook No. 395, 5th Edition* (Washington, D.C.: Nov. 2009).

[37] As previously mentioned, the proportion of cases in which job contacts were investigated ranged from less than 50 percent in 5 states, between 80 and 94 percent in 17 states, and between 95 and 100 percent in 16 states.

[38] GAO-14-704G.

definitive instructions to states on work search verification requirements, after the agency issues its planned letter to states about discontinuing the use of formal warning policies. As of May 2018, the agency said it plans to issue the letter on formal warning policies by the end of calendar year 2018. However, as previously stated, it has been nearly a year since DOL initially told us they were planning to issue the letter to states.

Effective monitoring of state compliance with the clarified work search verification requirements will also be important once DOL revises its BAM procedures. Federal internal control standards state that agency management should establish and operate monitoring activities to monitor the internal control system and evaluate the results. Monitoring states' responses could help ensure that DOL achieves its desired results. By providing clear direction to states about work search verification requirements and monitoring states' implementation of these requirements, DOL would have greater assurance that states are complying with its requirements.

CONCLUSION

The health of the UI program depends, in part, on the ability of states to control its benefit payments by accurately determining individuals' eligibility. Improper payments, including overpayments, in the UI program have led to billions of federal and state funds being used inappropriately.

Actively seeking work has generally been an eligibility requirement for individuals receiving unemployment benefits under federal law since 2012, but states have not consistently implemented the requirement for claimants in similar circumstances. States with formal warning policies reported lower work search overpayments not necessarily because they are better at ensuring claimants' compliance with requirements, but because they are not counting cases where claimants receive formal warnings as overpayments. Furthermore, although DOL determined in 2017 that states are not permitted to issue formal warnings rather than reporting an overpayment, it has not officially told states to stop using warnings. Without providing states with this information and monitoring their response, states will continue to report inconsistent information on the extent of work search overpayments.

State efforts to check whether claimants are meeting work search requirements also vary. Our evidence suggests that states making a greater effort to investigate work search activities tend to have lower overpayment rate estimates associated with this issue. However, some states are not investigating claimant-reported work search activities as part of their BAM audits despite DOL's procedures directing them to do so. Until DOL provides clear direction to states about verifying work search and monitors state compliance, DOL has little assurance that states are complying with its requirements.

RECOMMENDATIONS FOR EXECUTIVE ACTION

We are making the following four recommendations to the Department of Labor:

- The Assistant Secretary of DOL's Employment and Training Administration should provide states with information about its determination that the use of state formal warning policies is no longer permissible under federal law. (Recommendation 1)
- The Assistant Secretary of DOL's Employment and Training Administration should monitor states' efforts to discontinue the use of formal warning policies. (Recommendation 2)
- The Assistant Secretary of DOL's Employment and Training Administration should clarify information on work search verification requirements in its revised Benefit Accuracy Measurement procedures. The revised procedures should include an explanation of what DOL considers to be sufficient verification of claimants' work search activities. (Recommendation 3)
- The Assistant Secretary of DOL's Employment and Training Administration should monitor states' compliance with the clarified work search verification requirements. (Recommendation 4)

AGENCY COMMENTS

We provided a draft of this chapter to the Department of Labor (DOL) for review and comment. In its written comments, reproduced in appendix IV, DOL agreed with all four of our recommendations and stated that it would take action to address them. DOL also provided technical comments, which we incorporated as appropriate. Additionally, we provided excerpts of the draft chapter to state UI officials in the selected six states we included in our study. We incorporated their technical comments as appropriate.

As agreed with your office, unless you publicly announce the contents of this chapter earlier, we plan no further distribution until 30 days from the chapter date. At that time, we will send copies to the appropriate congressional committees, the Secretary of the Department of Labor, and other interested parties.

Sincerely yours,

Cindy Brown Barnes
Director, Education, Workforce, and Income Security Issues

APPENDIX I: ECONOMETRIC ANALYSIS OF ESTIMATED STATE WORK SEARCH OVERPAYMENT RATES

Data

We used the Department of Labor's (DOL) Unemployment Insurance Benefit Accuracy Measurement (BAM) data. The BAM program is designed to determine the accuracy of paid and denied claims for unemployment insurance (UI) in three major UI programs—state UI, Unemployment Compensation for Federal Employees (UCFE), and Unemployment Compensation for Ex-Service members (UCX). The BAM data covers claimants in the 50 U.S. states, the District of Columbia, and Puerto Rico.[39] Each week, state workforce agencies select random samples of paid and denied unemployment insurance claims (i.e., cases). State BAM investigators then audit these cases to determine whether the claimant was properly paid or was properly denied benefits in the week for which the claim was made (i.e., key week). The bases for determining whether paid and denied claims were accurate are federal and state law, regulations, and policy.

We used BAM cases for paid claims for all UI programs and all states for fiscal years 2013 through 2017.[40] The number of cases for each state is determined by DOL for each year. Cases are chosen randomly each week from the population of claims for that week. The normal weekly number of paid claims sampled in most states is 9, with a minimum of 6, for an annual sample of around 480 cases. For the 10 states with the smaller UI workloads, the normal weekly number of paid claims sampled is 7, with a minimum of 5, for an annual sample of around 360 cases.

For each paid claim case, the BAM data include variables describing the claimant, as well as information on their UI benefit year, separation from their last job, monetary eligibility, benefit payment history, employment services registration and work search, and the outcome of the BAM investigation. For cases for which BAM auditors identify errors, the BAM data also include information on the errors. In 2016, work search issues, benefit year earnings, and separation issues were the most common causes of reported overpayments:

- *Work search issues.* These occur when the state finds that claimants did not actively search for work during the key week. Federal law generally requires people receiving unemployment compensation to be actively searching for work. States have discretion to establish

39 We refer to the 50 U.S. states, the District of Columbia, and Puerto Rico collectively as "states."

40 DOL's fiscal year for reporting improper payment estimates covers July 1 through June 30 of the following year. For example, DOL's fiscal year 2017 improper payment estimate covers July 1, 2016 through June 30, 2017.

requirements for what constitutes active work search, and these requirements vary by state.

- *Benefit year earnings issues.* These occur when claimants have earnings that exceed the threshold for UI eligibility in their state or when these earnings are not properly reported.
- *Separation issues.* These occur when claimants are ultimately determined to be ineligible for UI due to disqualifying job separations, such as quitting a job without good cause or being discharged for misconduct under the state UI law.

Other causes of overpayments include incorrect reporting of wages used to calculate benefits, able and available to work issues, employment service registration issues, and other issues. For some cases, BAM investigators identify multiple errors with different causes. When this occurs, BAM investigators determine the overpayment amount associated with each cause.

BAM sample data is weighted to make inferences about the population. In accordance with DOL's method, we calculated the weight on each BAM sample case as (1) the number of unemployment compensation payments to claimants for the state and the week from which the BAM sample case was selected divided by, and (2) the number of completed BAM sample cases for that week, as long as there were two or more completed cases for the week.

Because each state followed a probability procedure based on random selections to pick cases, the BAM sample is only one of a large number of samples that they might have drawn. Since each sample could have provided different estimates, we express our confidence in the precision of the BAM sample's results using confidence intervals. For example, a 95 percent confidence interval is the interval that would contain the actual population value for 95 percent of the samples that could have been drawn. In some tables we provide the margin of error instead of the confidence interval, where the margin of error is the half-width of the confidence interval.

Our analysis sample consists of cases with no missing or invalid values of variables used in our analysis that also have positive sample weights. Our analysis sample includes 98.1percent of all cases.

Estimated Overpayment Rates Due to Failure to Meet Work Search Requirement

In accordance with DOL's method, the estimated overpayment rate is equal to the amount of UI benefits overpaid as a percentage of the total amount of UI benefits paid. The amount of UI benefits overpaid includes fraud, nonfraud recoverable, and nonfraud nonrecoverable overpayments; and overpayments from all causes and responsible parties. The amount overpaid excludes overpayments that DOL considers as technically proper. An overpayment may be considered technically proper by DOL under a finality rule, which generally means that too much time has passed between the decision to pay the claimant and the detection of the eligibility issue, or for some other reason. Our estimated work search overpayment rate is calculated using the same method as the official overpayment rate and is generally comparable to work search overpayment rates reported by DOL.[41]

More specifically, we used the BAM data to identify cases with overpayments and with overpayments due to work search, excluding formal warnings and other payments DOL considers to be technically proper. Next, we applied DOL's proration algorithm to allocate overpayment amounts for each error associated with a case so that the total amount of overpayments from all errors does not exceed the key week amount paid. Then, we calculated the total overpayment amount and work search overpayment amount for cases with overpayments and work search overpayments, respectively. Finally, we tracked the key week amount paid for each case. To estimate the work search overpayment rate for each state and fiscal year,

---

[41] For the purpose of this report, we refer to overpayments due to claimants' failure to meet work search requirements as work search overpayments.

we calculated the weighted sum of work search overpayment amounts as a percentage of the weighted sum of amounts paid.

Table 4. National and State Work Search Overpayment Rate Estimates, Fiscal Years 2013 through 2017

Percentage	2013	2014	2015	2016	2017
National work search overpayment rate estimate	2.4	3.9	2.9	4.1	4.5
	[2.2, 2.7]	[3.6, 4.2]	[2.7, 3.2]	[3.8, 4.5]	[4.1, 4.9]
State work search overpayment rate estimate					
Average	2.6	4.3	4.2	4.5	4.6
Minimum	0.0	0.0	0.0	0.0	0.0
10th percentile	0.0	0.0	0.0	0.0	0.0
25th percentile	0.1	0.3	0.4	1.2	0.4
Median	1.4	2.2	3.0	2.5	2.7
75th percentile	4.4	7.8	6.1	7.2	5.8
90th percentile	7.2	9.6	10.5	11.1	11.9
Maximum	10.8	18.2	15.8	26.7	40.7

Source: GAO analysis of the Department of Labor's Benefit Accuracy Measurement data. | GAO-18-486.

Notes: Work search overpayment rate estimates were calculated using cases in analysis sample. For the national work search overpayment rate estimate, 95 percent confidence intervals are in brackets. The margins of error associated with 95 percent confidence intervals for state work search overpayment rate estimates are no more than 4.9 percentage points each year.

Table 4 shows the estimated national work search overpayment rate, the average estimated state work search overpayment rate, and the median estimated state work search overpayment rate for each fiscal year. The national work search overpayment rate estimate has increased from 2.4 percent in 2013 to 4.5 percent in 2017. Over the same time period, the average state work search overpayment rate estimate has increased from 2.6 to 4.6 percent, and the median state work search overpayment rate estimate has increased from 1.4 percent to 2.7 percent.[42] Most states' work search

---

[42] The average state work search overpayment rate estimate in 2017 is statistically significantly different from the average state work search overpayment rate estimate in 2013 at the 5 percent level. The median state work search overpayment rate estimate in 2017 is not

overpayment rate estimates are less than 5 percent, but some states' rates are more than 10 percent.

Factors Associated with Work Search Overpayments

To identify state practices and other factors that may be associated with state work search overpayment rates, we reviewed DOL documents describing the BAM program and summarizing key features of states' UI programs, as well as research on factors associated with time claimants spend searching for employment. Based on our review, we identified factors that may be associated with work search overpayments that can be measured using variables in the BAM data:

- *Exemptions from work search requirements.* According to DOL, while federal law generally requires claimants to be actively seeking work, it does allow states to exempt claimants in some circumstances. For example, according to DOL, because states may not deny benefits to an individual in approved training, all states provide an exemption from the requirements to be able and available for work and conducting an active work search for any week the individual is in approved training. In addition, according to DOL, some states allow work search exemptions if the worker is union-attached and finds work through the union hall, or if a separation is classified as a temporary lay-off and there is a reasonable expectation that the worker will return to work soon. According to DOL, other state work search exemptions include that the worker has a specified start date for new employment, has jury duty, has a compelling personal reason, is in a labor dispute with the employer, is the victim of domestic violence, or labor market or other information indicates no suitable employment.

statistically significantly different from the median state work search overpayment rate estimate in 2013 at the 10 percent level.

- It is possible for a case with a claimant who indicated he or she was not required to search for work to have a work search error if the claimant provided an invalid reason for being exempt from his or her state's work search requirement. For example, the claimant may have said that he or she was a member of a union with a hiring hall and obtained employment through union referrals or that he or she had a definite recall date, and therefore, the work search requirement was waived. However, the BAM investigator's verification with the union found that the claimant was not in good standing, or the investigator's verification with the employer found that the claimant had no definite recall date. In such a situation, the claimant might be held ineligible for a failure to conduct an active work search because the exemption was invalid.
- *Claimant response.* According to DOL, the claimant interview anchors the BAM audit and is a major error detection point, and the claimant questionnaire is a required standard form. Claimants may provide information for the BAM audit either in person, over the phone, or via mail or some other method. Some claimants may not respond to the audit at all. For the period from 2013 to 2017, of the work search overpayments that BAM auditors detected in their BAM sample of cases, about 37 percent of cases were uncovered during the claimant interview.
- *State investigation of job contacts.* Claimants are asked to provide information about job contacts as evidence that they were actively searching for work as part of the required claimant questionnaire. In addition, even if the claimant does not respond to the BAM audit, job contacts may be available for BAM auditors to investigate if the state's continued claim process captured the claimant's work search information. BAM staff must investigate a sufficient number of contacts to establish whether the claimant has met the state's work search requirement. For the period from 2013 to 2017, of the work search overpayments that BAM auditors detected in the BAM sample of cases, about 45 percent were uncovered by investigating claimant-provided job contacts.

- *State use of formal warnings.* If the BAM audit of a case determines that the claimant's work search during the key week was not acceptable, the state might issue a formal warning to the claimant instead of finding that the claimant received a work search overpayment, and these cases are not included in the calculation of the work search overpayment rate for that state. Over the period from 2013 to 2017, of the BAM sample of cases for which work search errors were identified, state workforce agencies issued formal warnings for about 46 percent.
- *Claimant demographic and other characteristics.* Characteristics of claimants that are associated with the amount of time claimants spend searching for work include age, education, gender, length of time between initial claim and key week, and weekly benefit amount as a percentage of the normal weekly wage in the claimant's industry. To the extent that they affect time spent searching for work, these characteristics may also be associated with the likelihood of claimants receiving a work search overpayment.

Some factors that may be associated with work search overpayments cannot be measured using variables in the BAM data and, thus, are excluded from our analysis. Examples include:

- *Minimum number of work search activities.* According to DOL, the minimum number of work search activities required per week varies across states and can vary based on labor market conditions, which can, for example, produce different requirements in a rural area versus an urban area. However, some states do not specify a required number of work search activities and instead require that the number of work search activities be "reasonable," according to a DOL report.[43]

---

[43] Department of Labor, Employment and Training Administration, *2016 Comparison of State Unemployment Insurance Laws*.

- *Type of required employer contacts.* According to DOL, some states allow claimants to search for part-time work as well as full-time work, while others do not. In addition, according to DOL, some states specify that participation in reemployment services counts as a contact, and some states require claimants to make at least one contact through the state online system.
- *Frequency and method of reporting.* According to DOL, some states require weekly claimant reporting of work search activities, while others require bi-weekly reporting. In addition, according to DOL, some states require claimants to report online as part of their continued claim, while others require claimants to keep a log of their work search activities.

Econometric Mode

Our econometric model is the following:

$$\textit{work search overpayment rates}_{s,y} = \alpha + \beta * \textit{work search requireds}_{s,y} + \gamma_1 * \textit{n-person responses}_{s,y} + \gamma_2 * \textit{telephone responses}_{s,y} + \gamma_3 * \textit{mail, email, fax, or other responses}_{s,y} + \delta * \textit{contacts investigateds}_{s,y} + \phi_1 * \textit{low formal warning uses}_{s,y} + \phi_2 * \textit{moderate formal warning uses}_{s,y} + \phi_3 * \textit{requent formal warning uses}_{s,y} + X_{s,y}'\theta + \textit{year indicators} + \varepsilon_{s,y},$$

where s and y denote state and year, respectively, and the explanatory variables in the model are the following:

- *Work search required* is the estimated fraction of cases with claimants for whom work search is required, according to the BAM data.
- *In-person response*, telephone response, and mail, email, fax, or other response are the estimated fractions of cases with claimants who responded to the BAM audit in person, by telephone, or by mail, email, fax, or other method, respectively.
- *Contacts investigated* is the estimated fraction of cases for which BAM auditors investigated one or more job contacts.

- *Low, moderate, and frequent formal warning use* are binary indicator variables equal to 1 if the state issued a low, moderate, or high number of formal warnings in the fiscal year as a percentage of BAM cases with work search errors, respectively, and 0 otherwise. We defined low formal warning states as those that issued formal warnings for some but less than 25 percent of the cases with work search errors, moderate formal warning states as those that issued formal warnings for at least 25 percent but less than 75 percent of cases with work search errors, and high formal warning states as those that issued formal warnings for anywhere from 75 to 100 percent of cases with work search errors. The omitted group is states that issued no formal warnings during the fiscal year.
- *X* is a list of other characteristics of claimants that may be associated with work search, including the estimated distributions of cases across claimants' age groups, education levels, gender, length of time between initial claim and key week, and weekly benefit amount as a percentage of the normal weekly wage for their occupation.
- ε is an error term.
- The parameters of interest in our econometric model are β, γ_1, γ_2, γ_3, δ, ϕ_1, ϕ_2, and ϕ_3

The parameter β is an estimate of the change in the work search overpayment rate associated with a 1 percentage point increase in the fraction of cases with claimants who were required to search for work, all else being equal.

- The parameter γ_1 is an estimate of the change in the work search overpayment rate associated with a 1 percentage point increase in the fraction of cases with claimants who responded to the BAM audit in person, all else being equal. The parameters γ_2 and γ_3 are estimates of the change in the work search overpayment rate associated with a 1 percentage point increase in the fraction of cases with claimants who responded to the BAM audit by telephone and by mail, email, fax, or other method, respectively, all else being equal.

- The parameter ä is an estimate of the change in the work search overpayment rate associated with a 1 percentage point increase in the fraction of cases for which BAM auditors investigated one or more job contacts, all else being equal.
- The parameters ϕ_1, ϕ_2, and ϕ_3 are estimates of the changes in the work search overpayment rate associated with state issuance of a low, moderate, and high number of formal warnings, respectively, relative to states that issued no formal warnings.

Table 5. Summary of State Practices and Claimant Characteristics, Fiscal Years 2013 through 2017

	Average for fiscal year				
	2013	**2014**	**2015**	**2016**	**2017**
Percentage of cases with claimants required to search for work	76.8	76.9	77.6	78.9	78.3
Percentage of cases with claimants who responded to the BAM audit…					
…in-person	14.1	12.0	9.3	8.0	6.7
…by telephone	37.1	38.4	39.4	40.3	38.7
…by mail, email, fax, or some other method	41.9	41.7	42.8	42.1	44.0
Percentage of cases with claimants who did not respond to the BAM audit	6.9	7.9	8.5	9.7	10.7
Percentage of cases for which BAM auditors investigated job contacts	62.9	65.2	66.2	67.8	66.0
Percentage of cases with claimants who are…					
…age 14-24	7.3	6.7	6.1	5.5	5.1
…age 25-34	24.0	22.9	23.1	22.8	22.2
…age 35-44	21.9	22.0	21.9	21.6	22.1
…age 45-64	42.0	43.0	43.4	43.9	44.6
…age 65 and over	4.8	5.4	5.6	6.2	6.0
Percentage of cases with claimants who have…					
…no high school diploma or GED	12.2	11.8	11.3	11.3	10.2
…a high school diploma or GED	42.4	41.2	41.5	41.8	41.2
…some college or an associate's degree	30.3	30.6	30.6	30.1	30.1
…a bachelor's degree or more education	15.0	16.4	16.5	16.8	18.5
Percentage of cases with female claimants	41.2	42.6	41.3	40.6	41.4

	Average for fiscal year				
	2013	**2013**	**2013**	**2013**	**2013**
Percentage of cases with claimants who have received unemployment insurance benefits for...					
...0 to 4.9 weeks	10.6	7.4	8.2	7.8	11.2
...5 to 14.9 weeks	41.5	41.6	43.6	44.1	43.3
...15 to 26.9 weeks	31.0	32.3	30.0	30.2	28.9
...27 to 51.9 weeks	15.7	17.2	16.5	16.2	15.2
...52 weeks or more	1.2	1.5	1.7	1.8	1.4
Percentage of cases with claimants whose weekly benefit amount as a percentage of the normal weekly wage for their occupation is...					
...0 to 19.9 percent	6.5	7.0	6.1	7.5	7.6
...20 to 39.9 percent	30.5	31.0	31.6	30.9	32.0
Percentage of cases with claimants whose weekly benefit amount as a percentage of the normal weekly wage for their occupation is...					
...40 to 59.9 percent	44.5	44.1	44.0	43.4	42.9
...60 to 79.9 percent	15.3	14.8	15.0	15.1	14.4
...80 percent or more	3.2	3.1	3.2	3.2	3.0
Millions of weeks of paid claims	2.6	2.3	2.0	1.8	1.7

Source: GAO analysis of the Department of Labor's Benefit Accuracy Measurement data. | GAO-18-486.

Notes: Estimated average percentages were calculated using sample weights to reflect the sample design of the Benefit Accuracy Measurement data. All estimated average percentages have a margin of error no greater than plus or minus 1.3 percentage points at the 95 percent level of confidence.

Table 6. Summary of State Use of Formal Warnings, 2013-2017

	Fiscal year				
	2013	**2014**	**2015**	**2016**	**2017**
Number of states that issued formal warnings to...					
...0 BAM cases with work search errors	39	37	36	35	33
...0.1 to 24.9 percent of BAM cases with work search errors	2	3	1	2	2
...25 to 74.9 percent of BAM cases with work search errors	2	3	3	3	4
...75 to 100 percent of BAM cases with work search errors	9	9	11	12	13

Source: GAO analysis of the Department of Labor's Benefit Accuracy Measurement (BAM) data. | GAO-18-486.

Notes: For each state and fiscal year, the fraction of cases with work search errors that received formal warnings were calculated using unweighted numbers of cases. Using sample weights to reflect the sample design of the Benefit Accuracy Measurement data produces similar fractions of cases that lie within the same interval for each state and fiscal year.

For our baseline specification, we estimated the parameters using fractional response models to account for the unit interval range of the dependent variable, and we calculated standard errors clustered by state to allow for arbitrary correlation between the errors for a state in different years. To assess the robustness of our results, we also estimated the parameters using models with robust standard errors, using a single indicator variable to capture claimant response to the BAM audit versus nonresponse, and using linear models.

Table 5 shows descriptive statistics for the explanatory variables, other than formal warnings.

Table 6 shows descriptive statistics for states' use of formal warnings.

Caveats and Limitations

Our analysis is subject to several limitations, and the results we discuss below should be interpreted with caution.

- *No causality.* Our econometric approach can establish correlations between state work search overpayment rate estimates and the factors we analyzed, but it cannot establish causal relationships. This limitation is especially important when it comes to interpreting the relationship between work search overpayment rate estimates and the fraction of cases for which BAM auditors investigated job contacts. BAM investigations can only detect work search overpayments, not prevent them, because BAM investigators are reviewing cases after the payment has already been made. Preventing work search overpayments is the only way to reduce the work search overpayment rates. Thus, the relationship between investigation of claimant-provided contacts and work search overpayment rates likely reflects not a causal relationship but an equilibrium relationship in which claimants who know that their job contacts will be investigated are more likely to search for work, all else being equal.[44]

- *Nongeneralizability.* Our results do not generalize to other time periods with different labor market conditions, different rules and regulations about unemployment insurance, or other differences.
- *Omitted variables.* As discussed above, we have excluded from our models some state practices that may be associated with work search overpayments because those variables were not included in the BAM data. For example, we do not account for the fact that, according to DOL, some states require claimants to engage in more work search activities than other states, which could affect the likelihood that a claimant receives a work search overpayment. In addition, according to DOL, some states require claimants to report their work search activities in order to continue receiving benefits, which might prevent some work search overpayments from occurring. We have also likely excluded some relevant claimant characteristics as well. For example, total income for a claimant's household and a claimant's number of dependents may affect their work search efforts. However, variables describing a claimant's household income and composition are not included in the BAM data and thus are omitted from our analysis. To the extent that these factors are correlated with the factors we included, our estimates of the relationships between work search overpayment rates and the included factors could be biased.
- *Measurement error.* Our variables may have been measured with error, which could bias our coefficient estimates. If the measurement error is random, our coefficient estimates would be biased down, but if the measurement error is systematic, then we cannot say whether our coefficient estimates would be biased down or up.

---

[44] The intuition that claimants are more likely to search for work if they are more likely to get caught when they do not search for work is similar to the intuition that an increased likelihood of detection reduces tax evasion and other crime, all else being equal. See, for example, Gareth D. Myles, *Public Economics*, Cambridge: Cambridge University Press, 1995, and Aaron Chalfin and Justin McCrary, "Criminal Deterrence: A Review of the Literature," *Journal of Economic Literature*, vol. 55, no. 1, 2017, 5-48.

Results

Our baseline specification suggests that some state practices are associated with state work search overpayment rates estimates (see column 1 of Table 7). We used the 10 percent level of significance as our threshold for statistical significance because we have a relatively small number of observations (259).

- State work search overpayment rate estimates were higher in states with more cases with claimants who were required to search for work. A 1 percentage point increase in the fraction of cases with claimants required to search for work was associated with a 0.084 percentage point increase in the work search overpayment rate estimates on average, all else being equal.
- Work search overpayment rate estimates were lower in states with more cases for which the BAM auditors investigated one or more job contacts. A one percentage point increase in the fraction of cases for which the BAM auditors investigated contacts was associated with a 0.072 percentage point reduction in the work search overpayment rate on average, all else being equal.
- Compared to states that did not issue any formal warnings, work search overpayment rate estimates were higher in states that made low or moderate use of formal warnings but lower in states that issued formal warnings frequently. Work search overpayment rate estimates in states that were low and moderate users of formal warnings were 3.9 and 3.1 percentage points higher on average than those in states that issued no formal warnings, all else being equal. Work search overpayment rate estimates in states that were frequent users of formal warnings were 3.5 percentage points lower on average than those in states that issued no formal warnings.

Table 7. Estimated Changes in State Work Search Overpayment Rates Associated with State Practices and Claimant Characteristics, Fiscal Years 2013 to 2017

Percentage points	**Estimated change in the work search overpayment rate**	
	(1)	(2)
Percentage of cases with claimants required to search for work during the key week (relative to	0.084[c]	0.084[b]
cases with claimants who were exempt)	(0.046)	(0.038)
Percentage of cases with claimants who responded to the BAM audit...		
...in-person (relative to cases with claimants who did not respond to the BAM audit)	0.132	0.132[c]
	(0.087)	(0.069)
...by telephone (relative to cases with claimants who did not respond to the BAM audit)	0.124	0.124[c]
	(0.083)	(0.066)
... by mail, email, fax, or other method (relative to cases with claimants who did not respond to	0.157[c]	0.157[b]
the BAM audit)	(0.094)	(0.073)
Percentage of cases for which BAM auditors investigated job contacts (relative to cases for which	-0.072[b]	-0.072[b]
BAM auditors investigated no job contacts)	(0.032)	(0.029)
Percentage of cases with work search errors that received a formal warning...		
...0.1 to 24.9 percent (relative to states that issued no formal warnings)	0.039[a]	0.039[a]
	(0.012)	(0.013)
...25 to 74.9 percent (relative to states that issued no formal warnings)	0.031[b]	0.031[a]
	(0.014)	(0.011)
...75 percent or more (relative to states that issued no formal warnings)	-0.035[a]	-0.035[a]
	(0.007)	(0.005)
Percentage of cases with claimants who are...		
...age 25-34 (relative to cases with claimants age 14-24)	0.048	0.048
	(0.278)	(0.240)
...age 35-44 (relative to cases with claimants age 14-24)	0.197	0.197
	(0.238)	(0.232)
...age 45-64 (relative to cases with claimants age 14-24)	0.249	0.249
	(0.248)	(0.209)
...age 65 and over (relative to cases with claimants age 14-24)	0.132	0.132
	(0.270)	(0.257)

Table 7. (Continued)

Percentage points	Estimated change in the work search overpayment rate	
	(1)	(2)
Percentage of cases with claimants who have...		
...a high school diploma or GED (relative to cases with claimants with less than a high school	0.072	0.072
diploma or GED)	(0.113)	(0.088)
Percentage of cases with claimants who have...		
...some college/associates degree (relative to cases with claimants with less than a high school	0.192[c]	0.192[c]
diploma or GED)	(0.110)	(0.098)
...a bachelors degree or more (relative to cases with claimants with less than a high school	-0.016	-0.016
diploma or GED)	(0.118)	(0.101)
Percentage of cases with female claimants	0.013	0.013
	(0.072)	(0.052)
Percentage of cases with claimants who have received unemployment insurance benefits for...		
...5 to 14.9 weeks (relative to cases with claimants who have received unemployment insurance	-0.018	-0.018
benefits for 4.9 weeks or less at the time of the audit)	(0.146)	(0.128)
...15 to 26.9 weeks (relative to cases with claimants who have received unemployment	-0.128	-0.128
insurance benefits for 4.9 weeks or less at the time of the audit)	(0.125)	(0.111)
...27 to 51.9 weeks (relative to cases with claimants who have received unemployment	-0.261	-0.261[c]
insurance benefits for 4.9 weeks or less at the time of the audit)	(0.171)	(0.146)
...52 weeks or more (relative to cases with claimants who have received unemployment	-0.027	-0.027
insurance benefits for 4.9 weeks or less at the time of the audit)	(0.372)	(0.340)
Percentage of cases with claimants whose key week amount as a percent of the normal weekly wage in their occupation was...		
...20 to 39.9 percent (relative to cases with claimants whose key week amount was less than 20	0.259	0.259
percent of the normal weekly wage in their occupation)	(0.245)	(0.183)
...40 to 59.9 percent (relative to cases with claimants whose key week amount was less than 20	0.214	0.214
percent of the normal weekly wage in their occupation)	(0.178)	(0.131)
...60 to 79.9 percent (relative to cases with claimants whose key week amount was less than 20	0.257	0.257[c]
percent of the normal weekly wage in their occupation)	(0.188)	(0.147)

Percentage points	Estimated change in the work search overpayment rate	
	(1)	(2)
...80 percent or more (relative to cases with claimants whose key week amount was less than	0.244	0.244
20 percent of the normal weekly wage in their occupation)	(0.242)	(0.199)
Millions of weeks of paid claims	-0.000	-0.000
	(0.002)	(0.001)
Observations	259	259
Fiscal year indicators	Yes	Yes
Fractional response logit estimator	Yes	Yes
Standard errors clustered by state	Yes	Yes
Robust standard errors	No	No

Source: GAO analysis of the Department of Labor's Benefit Accuracy Measurement data. | GAO-18-486.

Notes: Average estimated marginal effects on state work search overpayment rates are derived from fractional response logit estimators with standard errors clustered by state (column 1) or robust standard errors (column 2). Work search overpayment rates and explanatory variables other than the indicators of formal warnings use are measured in decimals and range from 0 to 1. Indicators of formal warnings use are binary indicator variables.

[a]Statistically significant at the 1 percent level.

[b]Statistically significant at the 5 percent level.

[c]Statistically significant at the 10 percent level.

Our state-level analysis also suggests that some characteristics of cases are not associated with state work search overpayment rate estimates, but others are. State work search overpayment rate estimates were not significantly associated with the distribution of cases by claimant age, gender, duration of unemployment benefits receipt, or key week amount as a percentage of the normal weekly wage in their occupation, or with the number of cases. However, state work search overpayment rate estimates were higher in states with more cases with claimants with some college or an associate's degree relative to cases with claimants without a high school degree or GED. A one percentage point increase in the estimated fraction of cases with claimants with some college or an associate's degree was associated with a 0.192 percentage point increase in estimated work search overpayment rates on average, all else being equal.

To assess the sensitivity of our results, we estimated fractional response models with robust standard errors instead of clustered standard errors (see column (2) of Table 7). We also estimated fractional response models that replaced the fractions of cases by claimant response method with the fraction of cases with claimants who responded to the BAM audit by all methods combined, with both types of standard errors. Finally, we estimated linear models, also with both types of standard errors. While the direction and magnitude of the relationship between estimated work search overpayment rates and the fraction of cases with claimants required to search for work was generally similar across specifications, it was not always statistically significant. The direction, magnitude, and statistical significance of the relationship between estimated work search overpayment rates and the fraction of cases for which BAM auditors investigated job contacts was generally similar across specifications, with the exception of the linear model with clustered standard errors, where it was not statistically significant. The directions, magnitudes, and statistical significance of the relationship between estimated work search overpayment rates and estimated state formal warning use were generally similar across specifications.

APPENDIX II: ADDITIONAL BENEFIT ACCURACY MEASUREMENT DATA TABLES

This appendix contains several tables that show the underlying data used throughout this chapter, using the Department of Labor's Benefit Accuracy Measurement (BAM) data for fiscal years 2013 through 2017.

According to DOL, because the BAM data are based on a statistical survey, estimates produced from our analysis of the BAM data are subject to sampling and non-sampling errors. Sampling errors are errors that arise in a data collection process as a result of taking a sample from a population rather than using the whole population. Non-sampling errors are errors or biases that arise in a data collection process as a result of factors other than taking a sample, such as the timeliness of data collection, data entry errors, biased questions in fact-finding, biased decision-making, and inappropriate analysis and conclusions completed by state investigators or false or inaccurate information provided by survey respondents. We express our confidence in the precision of our results by reporting the margins of error associated with 95 percent confidence intervals. This is the interval that would contain the actual population value for 95 percent of the samples the respective agency could have drawn.

In addition, it may be misleading to compare one state's work search overpayment rates with another state's rates. According to DOL, no two states' written laws, regulations, and policies specifying eligibility conditions are identical, and differences in these conditions influence the potential for error.

The following tables and information are included in this appendix:

- **Table 8:** The estimated overpayment amounts for the Unemployment Insurance (UI) program by cause in fiscal year 2017 (also represented in Figure 2 in the letter portion).
- **Table 9:** The national work search overpayment rate estimates and dollar amounts for fiscal years 2013 through 2017 (also represented in Figure 3 in the letter portion).[45]
- **Table 10:** The work search overpayment rates estimates and dollar amount of work search overpayments in each state in fiscal year 2017, excluding cases where formal warnings were given.
- **Table 11:** The percentage of cases in which claimants were required to search for work and the percentage of those cases in which job contacts were investigated in each state in fiscal year 2017.
- **Table 12:** For states that issued formal warnings in 2017, the UI overpayment rate estimates excluding and including cases in which formal warnings were issued, and the difference in the dollar amount of overpayments if formal warnings were not used.

---

[45] For the purpose of this report, we refer to overpayments due to failure to meet work search requirements as work search overpayments.

Table 8. Estimated Overpayment Rates and Amounts by Cause, Fiscal Year 2017

Cause	Estimated rate (percentage of benefits paid)	Margin of error associated with 95 percent confidence interval	Estimated amount (dollars in millions)	Margin of error associated with 95 percent confidence interval (dollars in millions)
Benefit year earnings	3.1	0.4	958.7	110.2
Separation issues	2.1	0.3	639.2	103.3
Work search issues	4.5	0.4	1,363.9	115.2
All other issues	2.3	0.4	689.9	96.7

Source: GAO analysis of Department of Labor's Benefit Accuracy Measurement data. | GAO-18-486.

Note: This excludes formal warning cases, which are cases in which claimants who failed to search for work in one week were provided benefits.

Table 9. National Work Search Overpayment Rate Estimates and Amounts, Fiscal Years 2013 through 2017

Fiscal year	Estimated rate (percentage of benefits paid)	Margin of error associated with 95 percent confidence interval	Estimated amount (dollars in millions)	Margin of error associated with 95 percent confidence interval (dollars in millions)
2013	2.4	0.3	986.4	113.5
2014	4.0	0.4	1,460.1	127.8
2015	3.0	0.3	966.0	92.4
2016	4.2	0.4	1,303.0	116.5
2017	4.5	0.4	1,363.9	115.2

Source: GAO analysis of Department of Labor's Benefit Accuracy Measurement data. | GAO-18-486.

Note: This excludes formal warning cases, which are cases in which claimants who failed to search for work in one week were provided benefits.

Table 10. State Work Search Overpayment Rate Estimates and Amounts, Excluding Formal Warnings, Fiscal Year 2017

State	Work search overpayment rate estimates (percentage of benefits paid)	Margin of error associated with 95 percent confidence interval (percentage of benefits paid)	Amount of work search overpayment estimates (dollars in millions)	Margin of error associated with 95 percent confidence interval (dollars in millions)
Alaska	3.2	1.5	4.0	2.0
Alabama	2.8	1.6	5.1	3.0
Arkansas	0	0.8	0	1.1
Arizona	1.2	1.0	3.0	2.5
California	0.2	0.4	10.4	20.4
Colorado	6.3	2.3	30.2	11.2
Connecticut	14.8	3.7	94.3	24.6
District of Columbia	1.9	1.5	2.4	2.0
Delaware	0.1	0.3	0.1	0.2
Florida	0.9	0.9	3.3	3.3
Georgia	1.5	1.2	5.2	3.9
Hawaii	0.3	0.6	0.5	1.1
Iowa	0.8	0.8	3.5	3.6
Idaho	4.3	2.2	4.6	2.4
Illinois	4.0	1.8	71.5	31.9
Indiana	0	0.8	0	2.2
Kansas	17.5	3.5	33.2	7.1
Kentucky	2.0	1.3	5.7	3.6
Louisiana	0	0.8	0	1.6
Massachusetts	13.1	3.3	190.3	49.7
Maryland	8.5	2.6	44.8	14.0
Maine	6.6	2.4	6.3	2.3
Michigan	41.2	4.9	330.6	49.1
Minnesota	0.2	0.4	1.9	3.0
Missouri	0.2	0.4	0.5	1.1
Mississippi	2.7	1.4	2.3	1.2
Montana	4.8	2.5	5.2	2.8
North Carolina	15.1	3.3	32.3	7.4
North Dakota	7.3	2.8	10.5	4.1

Table 10. (Continued)

State	Work search overpayment rate estimates (percentage of benefits paid)	Margin of error associated with 95 percent confidence interval (percentage of benefits paid)	Amount of work search overpayment estimates (dollars in millions)	Margin of error associated with 95 percent confidence interval (dollars in millions)
Nebraska	5.8	2.7	4.2	2.0
New Hampshire	4.8	2.2	2.4	1.2
New Jersey	1.9	1.3	35.0	24.1
New Mexico	0.5	0.9	0.8	1.6
Nevada	4.1	1.8	11.9	5.1
New York	4.6	2.0	104.3	47.0
Ohio	7.6	2.8	69.6	26.0
Oklahoma	0.6	0.9	2.0	2.8
Oregon	7.0	2.5	33.5	12.4
Pennsylvania	0	0.8	0	16.0
Puerto Rico	0	0.8	0	1.1
Rhode Island	6.7	2.4	10.0	3.6
South Carolina	0	0.7	0	1.3
South Dakota	2.7	1.8	0.8	0.5
Tennessee	4.8	2.1	8.7	3.8
Texas	1.9	1.4	52.1	37.4
Utah	2.5	1.6	4.1	2.6
Virginia	2.3	1.4	8.8	5.2
Vermont	2.9	1.9	2.0	1.3
Washington	5.5	2.2	51.8	20.9
Wisconsin	12.7	3.2	59.5	16.0
West Virginia	0	0.7	0	1.4
Wyoming	0.3	0.5	0.3	0.4
United States	4.5	0.4	1363.9	115.2

Source: GAO analysis of Department of Labor's Benefit Accuracy Measurement data. | GAO-18-486.

Note: This excludes formal warning cases, which are cases in which claimants who failed to search for work in one week were provided benefits.

Table 11. Percentage of Cases with Claimants Required to Search for Work and Percentage for Which Job Contacts Were Investigated by State, Fiscal Year 2017

State	Cases with claimants required to search for work (percentage of cases)	Cases for which job contacts were investigated (percentage of cases with claimants required to search for work)	State	Cases with claimants required to search for work (percentage of cases)	Cases for which job contacts were investigated (percentage of cases with claimants required to search for work)
Alaska	80.1	96.3	Montana	47.6	98.2
Alabama	92.1	89.1	North Carolina	98.5	76.7
Arkansas	88.4	22.4	North Dakota	38.2	91.3
Arizona	99.0	99.6	Nebraska	57.6	99.5
California	81.0	53.6	New Hampshire	91.9	97.3
Colorado	79.9	76.4	New Jersey	78.7	31.4
Connecticut	91.3	54.3	New Mexico	91.1	99.8
District of Columbia	100.0	98.9	Nevada	88.4	48.9
Delaware	71.1	79.3	New York	75.2	48.8
Florida	96.6	99.1	Ohio	81.5	99.2
Georgia	85.5	90.5	Oklahoma	92.1	81.3
Hawaii	54.4	80.8	Oregon	89.5	95.8
Iowa	50.8	79.1	Pennsylvania	70.9	36.2
Idaho	71.6	99.4	Puerto Rico	82.9	91.1
Illinois	68.6	91.5	Rhode Island	77.9	88.6
Indiana	81.2	83.4	South Carolina	96.4	61.8
Kansas	84.2	76.3	South Dakota	56.3	54.0
Kentucky	80.0	78.3	Tennessee	76.3	95.8
Louisiana	89.4	97.3	Texas	93.1	80.3
Massachusetts	84.8	72.6	Utah	70.8	100.0
Maryland	85.6	88.0	Virginia	93.8	98.0
Maine	92.3	87.0	Vermont	67.3	92.9
Michigan	93.9	62.9	Washington	83.8	76.9
Minnesota	70.8	90.2	Wisconsin	48.9	92.6
Missouri	75.8	63.8	West Virginia	66.5	92.1
Mississippi	94.4	93.1	Wyoming	80.6	95.9
			United States	80.3	80.3

Source: GAO analysis of Department of Labor's Benefit Accuracy Measurement data. | GAO-18-486.

Table 12. Selected States' Overpayment Rate and Potential Overpayment Rate Estimates Factoring in Formal Warning Cases, Fiscal Year 2017

State	Number of formal warnings	Over payment rate estimate, excluding formal warnings	Margin of error associated with 95 percent con-fidence interval	Overpayment rate estimate, including formal warnings	Margin of error associated with 95 percent confidence interval	Difference in estimated over payment amount including and excluding formal warnings ($ in millions)	Margin of error associated with 95 percent confidence interval ($ in millions)
Arkansas	25	7.6	2.4	11.2	3.0	4.9	2.6
Arizona	1	9.3	2.6	9.6	2.6	0.7	1.4
Colorado	198	15.4	3.4	52.1	4.7	176.1	26.2
Connecticut	28	17.1	3.8	23.4	4.4	39.8	16.8
District of Columbia	65	11.4	3.2	26.7	4.7	19.6	5.3
Delaware	19	4.6	2.2	10.1	3.3	4.0	2.0
Iowa	73	8.0	2.5	19.0	3.6	47.5	12.7
Indiana	185	9.8	2.8	39.1	4.9	84.2	14.6
Louisiana	3	11.9	3.1	12.6	3.2	1.4	1.6
Maryland	2	16.6	3.4	16.7	3.4	1.0	1.9
Maine	22	10.8	2.9	15.4	3.5	4.4	2.1
Minnesota	12	8.4	2.5	10.8	3.0	19.2	14.7
Missouri	133	5.5	2.3	31.5	4.6	71.6	13.8
Nebraska	39	10.4	3.4	20.7	4.6	7.5	2.6
New Jersey	102	9.3	2.6	29.6	4.5	379.7	82.4
Nevada	137	13.0	3.1	37.7	4.5	71.7	13.0
New York	20	14.1	3.3	17.7	3.6	81.6	40.7
Pennsylvania	203	10.4	2.9	49.5	5.0	823.3	124.4
Vermont	61	7.2	2.8	22.1	4.7	10.2	3.0
United States	1328	12.0	0.7	18.0	0.8	1,848.6	161.0

Source: GAO analysis of Department of Labor's Benefit Accuracy Measurement data. | GAO-18-486.

Note: The estimated rates represent the percentage of Unemployment Insurance benefits paid.

APPENDIX III: SUMMARY OF SIX STATES' WORK SEARCH REQUIREMENTS FOR UNEMPLOYMENT INSURANCE CLAIMANTS

Work search requirements for Unemployment Insurance claimants vary by state. According to our review of program documents in our six selected states, the minimum number of work search activities required per week ranged from not specified to four. Three of the states limited the work search activities to applying for jobs or contacting employers in other ways and the three other states had broader definitions of what would qualify as a work search activity. See Table 13 below for a summary of the work search requirements, confirmed by state officials, for the six states included in our review.

Table 13. Summary of Selected States' Work Search Requirements for UI Claimants

State	Minimum number of work search activities required per week	Types of activities that qualify as work search activities	Claimant reporting of work search activities
Indiana	3	Work search activities can include, but are not limited to: visiting a job center, attending a professional networking group or a job fair, creating a LinkedIn account, applying for a job.	Not required to report specific work search activities when filing claims, but must keep a written record of work search activities and provide it to the state Unemployment Insurance (UI) agency upon request.
Mississippi	3	Contact three employers each week to apply for work. An application must be completed with at least one of the three employer contacts. Employer contacts can be made by phone, internet, in-person, or by sending applications/resumes.	Must report their work search activities online as part of filing weekly claims.

Table 13. (Continued)

State	Minimum number of work search activities required per week	Types of activities that qualify as work search activities	Claimant reporting of work search activities
Nevada	Not specified	Work search activities can include, but are not limited to: submitting job applications, participating in job search activities at a job center, using online networking websites and online job boards.	Encouraged to report work search activities online as part of filing weekly claims. Must keep a written record of work search activities and provide it to the state UI agency upon request.
New Jersey	3	Contact three different employers for each week. Employer contacts can be made by phone, internet, in-person, or by sending applications/resumes.	Not required to report specific work search activities when filing claims. Advised to keep a record of their work search activities that would be available upon request.
Pennsylvania	3	Submit two job applications and complete one work search activity. Work search activities can include, but are not limited to attending a job fair, searching for jobs in the state's online job bank, and posting a resume in the job bank.	Not required to report specific work search activities when filing claims, but must keep a written record of work search activities and provide it to the state UI agency upon request.
Utah	4	Contact employers that the claimant has not contacted before or contact a previously contacted employer about a newly listed job opening. Employer contacts can be made by phone, internet, in-person, or by sending applications/resumes.	Must keep a written record of work search activities and report the activities online as part of filing weekly claims.

Source: GAO review of information provided by state officials and confirmed by state officials. I GAO-18-486.

Note: The information provided in this table is not based on a review of state laws and regulations.

APPENDIX IV: COMMENTS FROM THE DEPARTMENT OF LABOR

U.S. Department of Labor

Employment and Training Administration
200 Constitution Avenue, N.W.
Washington, D.C. 20210

JUL 2 4 2018

Cindy S. Brown-Barnes
Director
Education, Workforce, and Income Security Issues
U.S. Government Accountability Office
441 G. Street, N.W.
Washington, D.C. 20548

Dear Ms. Brown-Barnes:

Thank you for the opportunity to review and comment on the Government Accountability Office's (GAO) draft report, "Unemployment Insurance: Actions Needed to Ensure Consistent Reporting of Overpayments and Claimants' Compliance with Work Search Requirements."

The Department appreciates GAO's efforts to describe the state of play regarding Unemployment Insurance (UI) work search requirements and formal warning policies. While the Federal-State UI program has made significant progress over the past six years implementing its strategic plan to reduce improper payments, certain essential program features continue to contribute to the UI program's improper payment rate.

As the Department noted in its response to GAO's interim report, "Unemployment Insurance: State Use of Warnings Related to Work Search Requirements Affects DOL's Improper Payment Estimates (GAO-18-133R)," failure to meet work search requirements is currently the largest root cause of UI overpayments. UI claimants are required to certify that they have met a state's work search requirements and document their work search in accordance with the state's law. Federal law requires that when an eligibility issue is detected, the claimant must receive notice and an opportunity to provide information before the state may stop paying benefits. Because there are fundamental due process requirements that prevent nonpayment of benefits, work search errors generally cannot be prevented before the payment must be made to the claimant.

Additionally, the definition of improper payments established by the Improper Payments Elimination and Recovery Act (IPERA) requires that the Department report those overpayments that result from statutory requirements as part of its overall improper payment rate. As a result, the UI program faces a difficult challenge in achieving a reduction in reported improper payments under the requirements of IPERA.

The Department is committed to supporting states' efforts to reduce overpayments in the UI program. We currently work with states to provide robust monitoring and technical assistance.

The Department has put forth legislative proposals to help states in addressing their improper payment rates, such as allowing states to retain a small portion of overpayment recoveries to use for additional work to address improper payments. The Department has also established the UI Integrity Center, a state-driven source of innovative program integrity strategies aimed at addressing UI improper payments and reducing fraud.

The Department agrees with GAO's recommendations. The Employment and Training Administration's Office of Unemployment Insurance will provide states with information about its determination that the use of state formal warning policies is no longer permissible under federal law, will monitor states' efforts to discontinue the use of formal warning policies, will clarify information on work search verification requirements in its revised Benefit Accuracy Measurement procedures, and will monitor states' compliance with clarified work search verification requirements.

Thank you for your review and recommendations.

Sincerely,

Rosemary Lahasky
Deputy Assistant Secretary

APPENDIX V: GAO STAFF ACKNOWLEDGMENTS

Staff Acknowledgments

Cindy Brown Barnes, Danielle Giese (Assistant Director), Cathy Roark (Analyst in Charge), Carl Barden, Rachel Beers, Deborah Bland, Beryl Davis, Holly Dye, Alex Galuten, Dana Hopings, Joel Marus, Phillip McIntyre, Sheila R. McCoy, Jean McSween, Courtney LaFountain, Stacy Spence, Almeta Spencer, Matt Valenta made significant contributions to this chapter.

In: Unemployment Insurance
Editor: Arlette Bolk
ISBN: 978-1-53614-937-1

Chapter 2

UNEMPLOYMENT INSURANCE: LEGISLATIVE ISSUES IN THE 115TH CONGRESS*

Julie M. Whittacker and Katelin P. Isaaks

SUMMARY

The 115th Congress continues to consider many issues related to the two major components of the unemployment insurance (UI) system: Unemployment Compensation (UC) and Extended Benefits (EB). This chapter provides short summaries of legislative proposals with respect to UI programs. It also gives a brief overview of the UI programs that may provide benefits to eligible unemployed workers. In addition, it briefly summarizes UI proposals included in the President's budget for FY2019.

President Trump signed H.J.Res. 42 on March 30, 2017 (P.L. 115-17). This Congressional Review Act (CRA) resolution negated 20 C.F.R. Part 620. This now-negated rule had set out the circumstances under which states were allowed to prospectively drug test UC claimants based upon the prevalence of drug testing in the occupations in which they were seeking employment. Additionally, President Trump signed P.L. 115-123, the Bipartisan Budget Act of 2018, on February 9, 2018. Among other

---

* This is an edited, reformatted and augmented version of Congressional Research Service Publication No. R44836, Updated May 11, 2018.

provisions, P.L. 115-123 includes two types of UI provisions: (1) codification of Reemployment Services and Eligibility Assessments (RESEAs) for UI beneficiaries, including funding and other requirements; and (2) a deferral of outstanding interest on federal UI loans for the U.S. Virgin Islands.

This chapter also describes UI legislation proposed in the 115th Congress that addresses the following:

- Rehiring UI beneficiaries and exhaustees—H.R. 3702 and H.R. 4470
- Vouchers and demonstration projects—H.R. 1091
- Additional UI benefits for certain energy workers—S. 987 and H.R. 3314
- Drug Testing—H.R. 3330

For a brief overview of UC, see CRS In Focus IF10336, *The Fundamentals of Unemployment Compensation*.

The unemployment insurance (UI) system has two primary objectives: (1) to provide temporary, partial wage replacement for involuntarily unemployed workers and (2) to stabilize the economy during recessions. In support of these goals, several UI programs provide benefits for eligible unemployed workers.

OVERVIEW OF UNEMPLOYMENT INSURANCE PROGRAMS

In general, when eligible workers lose their jobs, the joint federal-state Unemployment Compensation (UC) program may provide up to 26 weeks of income support through regular UC benefit payments. UC benefits may be extended for up to 13 weeks or 20 weeks by the Extended Benefit (EB) program if certain economic situations exist within the state.[1] Currently,

[1] For detailed information on each of these programs, see CRS Report RL33362, *Unemployment Insurance: Programs and Benefits*. Certain groups of workers may qualify for income support from additional unemployment insurance (UI) programs, including Trade Adjustment Assistance (TAA), Reemployment Trade Adjustment Assistance (RTAA), and Disaster Unemployment Assistance (DUA). Workers who lose their jobs because of international competition may qualify for income support through the TAA program or the RTAA (for certain workers aged 50 or older). Workers may be eligible to receive DUA benefits if they are not eligible for regular Unemployment Compensation (UC) and their unemployment may be directly attributed to a declared natural disaster. More information on the TAA and RTAA

although the UC and EB programs are both authorized, no state is in an active EB period.

Unemployment Compensation Program

The Social Security Act of 1935 (P.L. 74-271) authorizes the joint federal-state UC program to provide unemployment benefits under which most states provide up to a maximum of 26 weeks of UC benefits.[2] Former federal workers may be eligible for unemployment benefits through the Unemployment Compensation for Federal Employees (UCFE) program.[3] Former U.S. military service members may be eligible for unemployment benefits through the Unemployment Compensation for Ex-service members (UCX) program.[4] The Emergency Unemployment Compensation Act of 1991 (P.L. 102-164) provides that ex-service members be treated the same as other unemployed workers with respect to benefit levels, the waiting period for benefits, and benefit duration.

Although federal laws and regulations provide broad guidelines on UC benefit coverage, eligibility, and determination, the specifics regarding UC benefits are determined by each state. This results in essentially 53 different programs.[5] Generally, UC eligibility is based on attaining qualified wages and employment in covered work over a 12-month period (called a base period) prior to unemployment. All states require a worker to have earned a certain amount of wages or to have worked for a certain period of time (or

---

programs are in CRS Report R42012, *Trade Adjustment Assistance for Workers*. (The report is out of print, but is available to congressional clients from the author upon request.)

[2] For more details on these states with less than 26 weeks of UC available, see CRS Report R41859, *Unemployment Insurance: Consequences of Changes in State Unemployment Compensation Laws*. In addition, the maximum UC duration is 28 weeks in Montana and 30 weeks in Massachusetts. When EB benefits are available, any available UC benefits above 26 weeks are treated effectively as if they were EB payments.

[3] 5 U.S.C. §§8501-8508.

[4] 5 U.S.C. §§8521-8525. For more information on the Unemployment Compensation for Ex-service members (UCX) program, see CRS Report RS22440, *Unemployment Compensation (Insurance) and Military Service*.

[5] The District of Columbia, Puerto Rico, and the Virgin Islands are considered to be states under UC law.

both) within the base period to be eligible to receive any UC benefits. The methods states use to determine eligibility vary greatly. Most state benefit formulas replace approximately half of a claimant's average weekly wage up to a weekly maximum.[6] Additionally, each state's UC law requires individuals to have lost their jobs through no fault of their own, and recipients must be able to work, available for work, and actively seeking work.[7] These eligibility requirements help ensure that UC benefits are directed toward workers with significant labor market experience and who are unemployed because of economic conditions.

The UC program is financed by federal taxes under the Federal Unemployment Tax Act[8] (FUTA) and by state payroll taxes under the State Unemployment Tax Act (SUTA). The 0.6% effective net FUTA tax paid by employers on the first $7,000 of each employee's earnings (no more than $42 per worker per year) funds federal and state administrative costs, loans to insolvent state UC accounts, the federal share (50%) of EB payments, and state employment services.[9]

SUTA taxes on employers are limited by federal law to funding regular UC benefits and the state share (50%) of EB payments. Federal law requires that the state tax be on at least the first $7,000 of each employee's earnings (it may be more) and requires that the maximum state tax rate be at least

[6] For details on UC eligibility and benefits, see CRS Report RL33362, *Unemployment Insurance: Programs and Benefits*.

[7] In some cases a worker may be eligible for benefit based upon quitting a job for a "good cause" reason. In all states, individuals who leave their work voluntarily must meet the state's good cause requirements if they are not to be disqualified from receiving UC. In many states, good cause is explicitly restricted to reasons connected with the work, attributable to the employer, or involving fault on the part of the employer. (For those states, see Table 5.5 in U.S. Department of Labor (DOL), *2017 Comparison of State Unemployment Insurance Laws*, available at https://workforcesecurity.doleta.gov/unemploy/pdf/uilawcompar/ 2017/non monetary.pdf.)

[8] 23 U.S.C. §§3301-11.

[9] The Federal Unemployment Tax Act (FUTA) imposes a 6.0% gross tax rate on the first $7,000 paid annually by employers to each employee. Employers in states with programs approved by the federal government and with no delinquent federal loans may credit 5.4 percentage points against the 6.0% tax rate, making the minimum net federal unemployment tax rate 0.6%. Details on how delinquent loans affect the net FUTA tax are in CRS Report RS22954, The Unemployment Trust Fund (UTF): State Insolvency and Federal Loans to States.

5.4%. Federal law also requires each employer's state tax rate to be based on the amount of UC paid to former employees (known as "experience rating"). Within these broad requirements, each state has great flexibility in determining its SUTA structure. Generally, the more UC benefits paid out to its former employees, the higher the tax rate of the employer, up to a maximum established by state law. Funds from FUTA and SUTA are deposited in the appropriate accounts within the Unemployment Trust Fund (UTF).

Extended Benefit Program

The EB program was established by the Federal-State Extended Unemployment Compensation Act of 1970 (EUCA; P.L. 91-373) (26 U.S.C. §3304, note). EUCA may extend receipt of unemployment benefits (extended benefits) at the state level if certain economic conditions exist within the state. As of the date of this publication, EB was activated only in the U.S. Virgin Islands.[10]

Extended Benefit Triggers

The EB program is triggered when a state's insured unemployment rate (IUR) or total unemployment rate (TUR) reaches certain levels.[11] All states

---

[10] For the current EB trigger notice, select "Extended Benefits Trigger Notice" at https://ows.doleta.gov/unemploy/claims_arch.asp.

[11] The total unemployment rate (TUR) is the three-month average of the ratio of unemployed workers to all workers (employed and unemployed) in the labor market. The TUR is essentially a three-month average version of the unemployment rate published by the Bureau of Labor Statistics (BLS) and based on data from the BLS's monthly Current Population Survey (CPS). The insured unemployment rate (IUR) is the ratio of UC claimants divided by individuals in UC-covered jobs. In addition, the IUR uses a different base of workers in its calculations as compared with the TUR. The IUR excludes several groups used in TUR calculations: self-employed workers, unpaid family workers, workers in certain not-for-profit organizations, and several other, primarily seasonal, categories of workers. In addition to those unemployed workers whose last jobs were in the excluded employment category, the IUR excludes the following: those who have exhausted their UC benefits (even if they are receiving EB benefits); new entrants or reentrants to the labor force; disqualified workers whose unemployment is considered to have resulted from their own actions rather than from economic conditions; and eligible unemployed persons who do not file for benefits.

must pay up to 13 weeks of EB if the IUR for the previous 13 weeks is at least 5% and is 120% of the average of the rates for the same 13-week period in each of the two previous years. States may choose to enact two other optional thresholds. (States may choose one, two, or none.) If the state has chosen one or more of the EB trigger options, it would provide the following:

- Option 1—up to an additional 13 weeks of benefits if the state's IUR is at least 6%, regardless of previous years' averages.
- Option 2—up to an additional 13 weeks of benefits if the state's TUR is at least 6.5% and is at least 110% of the state's average TUR for the same 13 weeks in either of the previous two years; up to an additional 20 weeks of benefits if the state's TUR is at least 8% and is at least 110% of the state's average TUR for the same 13 weeks in either of the previous two years.

EB benefits are not "grandfathered" (phased out) when a state triggers "off" the program. When a state triggers "off" of an EB period, all EB benefit payments in the state cease immediately regardless of individual entitlement.[12]

The EB benefit amount is equal to the eligible individual's weekly regular UC benefits. Under permanent law, FUTA finances half (50%) of the EB payments and 100% of EB administrative costs.[13]

---

[12] EB benefits on interstate claims are limited to two extra weeks unless *both* the worker's state of residence (e.g., Texas) and the worker's state of previous employment (e.g., Louisiana) are in an EB period.

[13] The Tax Relief, Unemployment Insurance Reauthorization, and Job Creation Act of 2010, P.L. 111-312, as amended (the final time by P.L. 112-240), made technical changes to certain triggers in the EB program. These changes allowed states to temporarily use lookback calculations based on three years of unemployment rate data (rather than the permanent-law lookback of two years of data) as part of their mandatory IUR and optional TUR triggers if states would otherwise trigger off or not be on a period of EB benefits. Using a two-year versus a three-year EB trigger lookback was an important adjustment at the time of the signing of P.L. 111-312 (December 17, 2010) because many states were likely to trigger off of their EB periods despite high, sustained—but not increasing—unemployment rates. For more information on these state law changes, see CRS Report R41859, *Unemployment Insurance: Consequences of Changes in State Unemployment Compensation Laws*. The authorization for the temporary EB trigger modifications expired the week ending on or before December 31, 2013.

States fund the other half (50%) of EB benefit costs through their SUTA.[14]

Unemployment Insurance Benefits and the Sequester

The sequester order required by the Budget Control Act of 2011 (BCA; P.L. 112-25) and implemented on March 1, 2013 (after being delayed by P.L. 112-240), affected some but not all types of unemployment insurance expenditures. Regular UC, UCX, and UCFE payments are not subject to the sequester reductions. EB, EUC08 (when it available), and most forms of administrative funding are subject to the sequester reductions.[15]

FY2018 Sequester of Unemployment Insurance Benefits

The FY2018 sequestration order requires a 6.6% reduction in all nonexempt nondefense mandatory expenditures, but no sequestration reductions are applicable to discretionary programs, projects, and activities.[16] As a result, EB expenditures are required to be reduced 6.6% (only on the federal share of EB benefits) for weeks of unemployment during

[14] P.L. 111-5, the American Recovery and Reinvestment Act of 2009 (most recently amended by P.L. 112-240, the American Taxpayer Relief Act of 2012), temporarily changed the federal-state funding arrangement for the EB program. The FUTA financed 100% of EB benefits from February 17, 2009, through December 31, 2013. The one exception to the 100% federal financing was for those "non-sharable" EB benefits (work not subject to FUTA taxes such as state and local government employment). Those non-sharable benefits continued to be 100% financed by the former employers.

[15] See CRS Report R42972, Sequestration as a Budget Enforcement Process: Frequently Asked Questions.

[16] Office of Management and Budget (OMB), *OMB Report to the Congress on the Joint Committee Sequestration for Fiscal Year 2018*, May 23, 2017, https://www.whitehouse.gov/sites/whitehouse.gov/files/omb/sequestration_reports/2018_jc_sequestration_report_may2017_potus.pdf.

FY2018.[17] As of the date of this publication, EB was activated only in the U.S. Virgin Islands.[18]

FY2017 Sequester of Unemployment Insurance Benefits

The FY2017 sequestration order required a 6.9% reduction in all nonexempt nondefense mandatory expenditures, but no sequestration reductions are applicable to discretionary programs, projects, and activities.[19] Therefore, the sequestration order required that EB expenditures be reduced by 6.9% (only on the federal share of EB benefits) for weeks of unemployment beginning on October 8, 2016, through September 30, 2017.[20] However, EB was not activated in any state during FY2017.[21]

State Fiscal Concerns Alleviating State Unemployment Compensation Stress

If a recession is deep enough and if state unemployment tax (SUTA) revenue is inadequate for long periods of time, states may have insufficient funds to pay for UC benefits. Federal law, which requires states to pay these benefits, provides a loan mechanism within the UTF framework that an

---

[17] For details, see Employment and Training Administration, U.S. Department of Labor, *Unemployment Insurance Program Letter*, UIPL 6-18, March 30, 2018, https://wdr.doleta.gov/directives/attach/UIPL/UIPL_6-18_Acc.pdf.

[18] For the current EB trigger notice, select "Extended Benefits Trigger Notice" at https://ows.doleta.gov/unemploy/ claims_arch.asp.

[19] Office of Management and Budget (OMB), *OMB Report to the Congress on the Joint Committee Sequestration for Fiscal Year 2017*, February 9, 2016, https://www.irs.gov/pub/whistleblower/2017_jc_sequestration_report_house.pdf.

[20] For details, see Employment and Training Administration, U.S. Department of Labor, *Unemployment Insurance Program Letter*, UIPL 9-17, January 19, 2017, https://wdr.doleta.gov/directives/attach/UIPL/UIPL_09-17_Acc.pdf.

[21] For the historical EB trigger notices, select "Extended Benefits Trigger Notice" and the years of interest at https://ows.doleta.gov/unemploy/claims_arch.asp.

insolvent state may opt to use to meet its UC benefit payment obligations.[22] States must pay back these loans. If the loans are not paid back quickly (depending on the timing of the beginning of the loan period), states may face interest charges, and states' employers may face increased net FUTA rates until the loans are repaid.[23]

As of February 18, 2018, California and the Virgin Islands both had outstanding loans. California owed $1.2 billion and the Virgin Islands owed$75.8 million to the federal accounts within the UTF.[24]

PRESIDENT'S BUDGET PROPOSAL FOR FY2019

The President's budget for FY2019 proposes changes to several aspects of the UI system.[25] It would create a new required standard for state account balances within the UTF. The President's FY2019 budget also proposes to make funding for Reemployment Services and Eligibility Assessments (RESEA) permanent beginning in 2020, and to make these assessments mandatory for 50% of UC beneficiaries.[26] Additionally, the proposal would create a new benefit entitlement for paid parental leave financed through state unemployment taxes. Finally, the President's budget for FY2018 proposes a set of additional integrity measures, including offsetting Social

---

[22] Federal UC law does not restrict the states from using loan resources outside of the UTF. Depending on state law, states may have other funding measures available and may be able to use funds from outside of the UTF to pay the benefits (such as issuing bonds).

[23] Details on how states may borrow federal funds to pay for UC benefits are in CRS Report RS22954, *The Unemployment Trust Fund (UTF): State Insolvency and Federal Loans to States*.

[24] U.S. Department of the Treasury, Bureau of Public Debt, *Title XII Advance Activities Schedule*, February 15, 2018, at http://www.treasurydirect.gov/govt/reports/tfmp/tfmp_advactivities sched.htm.

[25] The President's detailed budget proposal for UC in FY2019 is accessible at https://www.dol.gov/sites/default/files/budget/2019/CBJ-2019-V1-07.pdf. The President's budget for FY2018 included substantively similar UC proposals and is accessible at https://www.dol.gov/sites/default/files/CBJ-2018-V1-07.pdf.

[26] See the section in this report on "RSEA Provisions in Section 30206 of P.L. 115-123" for a description of RESEA changes subsequently enacted under P.L. 115-123, the Bipartisan Budget Act of 2018.

Security Disability Insurance (SSDI) benefits for concurrent receipt of UI benefits.

New Minimum Account Balance for State UTF Accounts

The President's budget proposal for FY2019 would require states to maintain a UTF account balance of at least 50% of the state's Average High Cost Multiple[27] (AHCM). The proposal would alter the rules for calculating the net FUTA rate, requiring a higher net FUTA rate on a state's employers if that state maintained an AHCM of less than 0.5 on January 1 of two or more consecutive years. The additional FUTA revenue would be deposited into the state UTF account and would be terminated once the state met the 0.5 AHCM criteria.[28]

Mandatory RESEA Services

The President's budget proposal for FY2019 would create permanent and mandatory RESEA program funding, beginning in 2019. States would be required to provide reemployment services and eligibility assessments to 50% of UC claimants as well as to 100% of Unemployment Compensation for Ex-Service members (UCX) claimants.[29] (Just prior to the February 12,

[27] The average high-cost multiple (AHCM) is the ratio of actual UTF account balances to the average of the three highest years of benefit payments experienced by the state over the past 20 years. Presumably, the average of the three highest years' outlays would be a good indicator of potential expected UC payments if another recession were to occur. Under these assumptions, if a state had saved enough funds to pay for an average high year of UC benefit activity, its AHCM would be at least 1.0.

[28] For the current AHCM in each state, see the last column of Table 1 in U.S. Department of Labor, Office of Unemployment Insurance, *State Unemployment Insurance Trust Fund Solvency Report*, Washington, DC, March 2017, https://ows.doleta.gov/unemploy/docs/trustFundSolvReport2017.pdf.

[29] Under current law, due to changes made by the Emergency Unemployment Compensation Act of 1991 (P.L. 102- 164), states are required to treat former military service members the same as other unemployed workers with respect to UC benefit levels, the waiting period for benefits, and benefit duration. For details on UCX, see CRS Report RS22440, *Unemployment Compensation (Insurance) and Military Service*.

2018 release of the President's budget proposal for 2019, Section 30206 of P.L. 115-123, the Bipartisan Budget Act of 2018 (enacted February 9, 2018) codified RESEA. See the section in this chapter on "P.L. 115-123" for a summary of the enacted RESEA provisions.)

Paid Family Leave Benefit

The President's budget proposal for FY2019 would require states to establish a paid parental leave benefit by 2020 using the UC program as its administrative framework. States would be required to provide six weeks of benefits to a worker on leave or otherwise absent from work for the birth or adoption of the worker's child.[30] States would have discretion to determine the parameters of eligibility and financing for this new paid parental leave benefit.

UI Program Integrity

Requirements to Use Particular Data Sources for Program Integrity

The President's 2019 budget includes additional integrity measures that would require states to use three specific data sources to confirm an individual's eligibility for UC benefits: State Information Data Exchange System (SIDES), the National Directory for New Hires (NDNH), and the Prisoner Update Processing System.[31]

---

[30] It is not clear if this proposal creates any new entitlement to job-protected leave itself; rather, it appears to create a new entitlement to income replacement while an individual is taking parental leave. For information on (1) states that currently operate state paid family leave insurance programs, including California, Rhode Island, and New Jersey, as well as (2) states that have enacted paid family leave insurance programs, but which are not yet fully implemented and paying benefits (e.g., New York, District of Columbia, and Washington State), see CRS Report R44835, *Paid Family Leave in the United States*.

[31] States currently have the federal authority to use these data sources, but their use is not mandatory.

Additional Integrity Proposals

The proposal would create several additional integrity measures. These include

- giving the Labor Secretary authority to implement new corrective action measures in response to poor state administrative performance within the program;
- allowing states to retain up to 5% of UC overpayments for program integrity use;
- requiring states to deposit all UC penalty and interest payments into a special state fund, with these funds required to be used for improving state UI administration as well as providing reemployment services for UI claimants;[32] and
- offsetting SSDI benefits to account for concurrent receipt of UI benefits.[33]

Proposed Rescission of Expired Temporary Extended Railroad Unemployment Benefits

On May 8, 2018, the Trump Administration submitted to Congress a proposal for 38 rescissions of budget authority. In their transmission, the Office of Management and Budget stated that these rescissions were transmitted pursuant to Section 1012 of the Congressional Budget and Impoundment Control Act of 1974 (2 U.S.C. 683).[34] Included in this

[32] In addition, under this proposal, states with high improper payment rates would be required to spend a portion of the UC penalty and interest payments funds on program integrity activities.

[33] For a discussion of legislative proposals on this issue introduced in the 114th Congress, see the section on "Concurrent Receipt of SSDI and UI Benefits" in CRS Report R43993, *Unemployment Insurance: Legislative Issues in the 114th Congress*. For general background on the issue of concurrent receipt of SSDI and UI, see CRS Report R43471, *Concurrent Receipt of Social Security Disability Insurance (SSDI) and Unemployment Insurance (UI): Background and Legislative Proposals*.

[34] The rescission transmittal (rescission proposal no. R18-1) is available on the White House website at https://www.whitehouse.gov/wp-content/uploads/2018/05/POTUS-Rescission-Transmittal-Package-5.8.2018.pdf.

proposal was a rescission of $132,612,397 from the unexpended remainder of a $175 million appropriation contained in P.L. 111-92 for a temporary program of extended Railroad unemployment benefits.[35] These temporary mandatory benefits were originally created in 2008 (P.L. 111-5, Title II, Section 2003) and the authority for the benefits expired on December 31, 2013 (P.L. 112-240, Title V, Section 504).

ENACTED LAWS IN THE 115TH CONGRESS

Congressional Review Act: Disapproval of Unemployment Compensation Drug Testing Regulations (H. J. Res. 42/P.L. 115-17)

On March 31, 2017, President Donald Trump signed H. J. Res. 42/P.L. 115-17. This Congressional Review Act (CRA) resolution negated 20 C.F.R. Part 620.[36] This rule had set out the circumstances under which states were allowed to prospectively drug test UC claimants based upon the prevalence of drug testing in the occupations in which they were seeking employment.[37] Since there are no longer any lists of occupations that require drug testing within the UC sections of the *Code of Federal Regulations* (on account of P.L. 115-17), this ability to prospectively test UC claimants based upon occupation is no longer available to states. Without this rule, states

---

[35] For summary information on the separate unemployment benefits available under the Railroad Unemployment Insurance Act (RUIA), see CRS In Focus IF10481, *Railroad Retirement Board: Retirement, Survivor, Disability, Unemployment, and Sickness Benefits*.

[36] See CRS Report R43992, The Congressional Review Act (CRA): Frequently Asked Questions.

[37] Section 2105 of the Middle Class Tax Relief and Job Creation Act of 2012 (P.L. 112-96; February 22, 2012) amended federal law to permit states to conduct two types of drug testing: (1) drug testing of UC applicants who were discharged from employment with their most recent employer (as defined under state law) for unlawful drug use (this remains available to states); and (2) drug testing of UC applicants for whom suitable work (as defined under state law) is available only in an occupation that regularly conducts drug testing, as determined under regulations issued by the Secretary of Labor. (Because there are no regulations in effect with the passage of P.L. 115-17, this option is not currently available to states.)

may drug test UC claimants only if they were discharged from employment because of either unlawful drug use or for refusing a drug test.[38]

S. J. Res. 23, introduced by Senator Ted Cruz on February 16, 2017, proposed measures identical to H. J. Res. 42.

The Bipartisan Budget Act of 2018 (P.L. 115-123)

On February 9, 2018, President Donald Trump signed the Bipartisan Budget Act of 2018 (P.L. 115-123). Among other provisions, P.L. 115-123 includes two UI-related changes. First, Section 20801 of P.L. 115-123 authorizes a deferral of interest payments on an outstanding federal UI loan for the U.S. Virgin Islands (USVI). Second, Section 30206 of P.L. 115-123 codifies Reemployment Services and Eligibility Assessments (RESEAs) for UI beneficiaries into Title III of the Social Security Act (SSA) and provides an allocation formula for the funds and other requirements.

Deferral of Interest Payments for USVI in Section 20801 of P.L. 115-123

Two major disaster declarations were announced by the Federal Emergency Management Agency (FEMA) for the U.S. Virgin Islands in September 2017.[39] This provision responds to the resulting economic conditions, including increased unemployment, in the USVI in the aftermath of Hurricanes Irma and Maria. Under this provision, the deadline for USVI's payment of interest on a federal UI loan that was due on September 29, 2017, was extended and is not due until September 28, 2018. Additionally, no

---

[38] Prior to issuing the final rule on this issue, DOL released guidance to states on drug testing of UC applicants who were discharged from employment with their most recent employer because of unlawful drug use or for refusing drug testing; this guidance remains in effect. U.S. DOL, Unemployment Insurance Program Letter (UIPL), No. 1-15, "Permissible Drug Testing of Certain Unemployment Compensation Applicants Provided for in Title II, Subtitle A of the Middle Class Tax Relief and Job Creation Act of 2012," October 4, 2014, available at https://wdr.doleta.gov/ directives/attach/UIPL/UIPL-1-15_Acc.pdf.

[39] See https://www.fema.gov/disaster/4335 and https://www.fema.gov/disaster/4340.

interest will accrue on this outstanding interest payment during the deferral period.[40]

RESEA Provisions in Section 30206 of P.L. 115-123

RESEA grants have been directed to states by U.S. Department of Labor (DOL) since 2005 through discretionary appropriations.[41] Section 30206 of P.L. 115-123 codifies the authority for DOL to administer a RESEA program.[42] It also sets out various requirements for states to use certain types of evidence-based interventions for UI claimants under RESEA as well as allocates discretionary funding for RESEA across three categories (base funding, outcome payments, and research and technical assistance). Under this law, state RESEA programs must include reasonable notice and accommodations to participating UI beneficiaries.

LEGISLATIVE PROPOSALS IN THE 115TH CONGRESS

Rehiring UI Beneficiaries and Exhaustees

Representative David McKinley introduced the Manufacturing Economic Recovery Act of 2017, H.R. 3702. The bill, among other items, would create a permanent work opportunity tax credit for hiring a full-time employee in a manufacturing facility located in the United States and include an increased credit for hiring individuals receiving unemployment compensation.

---

[40] For background on federal UI loans, see the section in this report on "State Fiscal Concerns Alleviating State Unemployment Compensation Stress."

[41] For additional background, see CRS Report R43044, Expediting the Return to Work: Approaches in the Unemployment Compensation Program.

[42] The law created a new Section 306 of the Social Security Act. Just over a month later, on March 23, 2018, the Consolidated Appropriations Act, FY2018 (P.L. 115-141), provided $2.6 billion from the UTF for grants to states for the administration of state unemployment insurance laws as authorized under title III of the Social Security Act (including not less than $120 million for RESEA and UC improper payment reviews, and to provide reemployment services and referrals to training, as appropriate) and provided that such activities would not be subject to the newly-created section 306 of the Social Security Act for that fiscal year (FY2018).

Delegate Eleanor Holmes Norton introduced the Reducing Long-Term Unemployment Act, H.R. 4470. The bill would suspend employment and railroad retirement taxes for employers who hired unemployed individuals through 2018. The aggregate reduction in taxes from such suspension would be limited to $5,000 per employee.

Vouchers and Demonstration Projects

Representative James Renacci sponsored H.R. 1091, the Flexibility to Promote Reemployment Act. The bill would make a number of changes to the state UC demonstration projects created by the Middle Class Tax Relief and Job Creation Act of 2012 (P.L. 112-96).[43] The bill would extend the time period that the (now-expired) state demonstration projects could be approved by DOL through December 31, 2021 (P.L. 112-96 authorized these demonstration projects through December 31, 2015), as well as expanded the existing authority for state UC demonstration projects by authorizing 10 states per year to conduct approved demonstration projects (the original, expired authority was only for 10 states total). H.R. 1091 would also revise state UC demonstration project requirements, including removing a requirement that any direct disbursements paid to employers for hiring UC claimants not exceed an individual's UC weekly benefit amount and requiring that DOL approve state applications for UC demonstration projects based on the order of receipt. Additionally, the bill would transfer the responsibility for the state UC demonstration project impact evaluation from the states, as under the now-expired demonstration authority, to DOL and would require a specific procedure for termination of the state UC demonstration project by DOL.

[43] For more details on these state UC demonstration projects, as authorized under 42 U.S.C. §505, see CRS Report R41662, *Unemployment Insurance: Legislative Issues in the 112th Congress*.

Unemployment Benefits for Energy Workers

Senator Jeff Merkley and Representative Jared Polis introduced S. 987 and H.R. 3314, the 100 by '50 Act, respectively. Among other provisions, these bills would allow states to provide additional, temporary, federally funded UI benefits to individuals who have exhausted all UI benefits (regular UC benefits and any other UI benefit available—e.g., EB benefits); who are certified as workers adversely affected by a transition away from fossil fuels and into clean and renewable energy by the year 2050; and who are receiving certain adjustment assistance provided through this proposal.

Drug Testing[44]

Representative Earl Carter sponsored H.R. 3330, the Ensuring Quality in the Unemployment Insurance Program (EQUIP) Act. The bill would require any UC applicant to complete a substance abuse risk assessment. If the applicant had been deemed high-risk, the applicant would have to pass a controlled substances test to receive UC benefits. Those who did not pass the test would be ineligible for benefits for 30 days and then would have to be retested to determine eligibility.

---

[44] For a legal analysis of required drug testing, see CRS Report R42326, Constitutional Analysis of Suspicionless Drug Testing Requirements for the Receipt of Governmental Benefits.

In: Unemployment Insurance
Editor: Arlette Bolk
ISBN: 978-1-53614-937-1

Chapter 3

UNEMPLOYMENT INSURANCE: LEGISLATIVE ISSUES IN THE 114TH CONGRESS*

Julie M. Whittaker and Katelin P. Isaacs

SUMMARY

The 114th Congress considered many issues related to unemployment insurance (UI) programs: Unemployment Compensation (UC), the temporary, now-expired Emergency Unemployment Compensation (EUC08), and Extended Benefits (EB). This chapter gives a brief overview of the UI programs that may provide benefits to eligible unemployed workers. In addition, it briefly summarizes the President's budget proposal for FY2017.

The National Defense Authorization Act for Fiscal Year 2016, P.L. 114-92, altered certain conditions for individuals to receive Unemployment Compensation for Former Service members (UCX).

This chapter also describes UI legislation proposed in the 114th Congress that addressed:

---

* This is an edited, reformatted and augmented version of Congressional Research Service, Publication No. R43993, dated April 28, 2017.

- Concurrent receipt of Social Security Disability Insurance (SSDI) and UI benefits—S. 343, S. 499, H.R. 5919, H.R. 918, and S. 2005
- UI program integrity—H.R. 2503 and H.R. 2512
- Unemployment Compensation for Former Service members (UCX)—P.L. 114-92, S. 1376, and H.R. 1735
- Drug testing—H.R. 1136, H.R. 2148, and H.R. 5945
- Rehiring UI beneficiaries and exhaustees—H.R. 481, H.R. 2265, H.R. 2721, H.R. 3555, H.R. 3622, H.R. 4593, H.R. 4973 and S. 1517
- Reauthorization of EUC08—H.R. 2721 and H.R. 3555
- Vouchers and demonstration projects—H.R. 2509, H.R. 2721, and H.R. 3555
- Job training and education—H.R. 2219
- Relocation Subsidies—H.R. 2755
- Short-time Compensation (STC)—H.R. 2721, H.R. 3555, H.R. 5408, and S. 1902
- New benefits for certain energy workers—H.R. 5669 and S. 2398
- Domestic violence—H.R. 3841 and S. 2208

For a brief overview of UC, see CRS In Focus IF10336, *The Fundamentals of Unemployment Compensation*.

The unemployment insurance (UI) system has two primary objectives: (1) to provide temporary, partial wage replacement for involuntarily unemployed workers and (2) to stabilize the economy during recessions. In support of these goals, several UI programs provide benefits for eligible unemployed workers.

Overview of Unemployment Insurance Programs

In general, when eligible workers lose their jobs, the joint federal-state Unemployment Compensation (UC) program may provide up to 26 weeks of income support through regular UC benefit payments. UC benefits may be extended for up to 13 weeks or 20 weeks by the Extended Benefit (EB) program if certain economic situations exist within the state.[1] During previous Congresses, the temporarily authorized Emergency Unemployment Compensation (EUC08) program provided additional weeks of benefits (depending on the date, from 13 weeks to 53 weeks). EUC08 benefits expired on December 28, 2013, and are no longer authorized. Currently, although the UC and EB programs are authorized, no state is in an active EB period.

Unemployment Compensation Program

The Social Security Act of 1935 (P.L. 74-271) authorizes the joint federal-state UC program to provide unemployment benefits under which most states provide up to a maximum of 26 weeks of UC benefits.[2] Former federal workers may be eligible for unemployment benefits through the Unemployment Compensation for Federal Employees (UCFE) program.[3] Former U.S. military service members may be eligible for unemployment benefits through the Unemployment Compensation for Ex-service members (UCX) program.[4] The Emergency Unemployment Compensation Act of 1991 (P.L. 102-164) provides that ex-service members be treated the same

---

[1] For detailed information on each of these programs, see CRS Report RL33362, *Unemployment Insurance: Programs and Benefits*. Certain groups of workers may qualify for income support from additional unemployment insurance (UI) programs, including Trade Adjustment Assistance (TAA), Reemployment Trade Adjustment Assistance (RTAA), and Disaster Unemployment Assistance (DUA). Workers who lose their jobs because of international competition may qualify for income support through the TAA program or the RTAA (for certain workers aged 50 or older). Workers may be eligible to receive DUA benefits if they are not eligible for regular Unemployment Compensation (UC) and their unemployment may be directly attributed to a declared natural disaster. For more information on the TAA and RTAA programs, see CRS Report R42012, *Trade Adjustment Assistance for Workers*.

[2] For more details on these states with less than 26 weeks of UC available, see CRS Report R41859, *Unemployment Insurance: Consequences of Changes in State Unemployment Compensation Laws*. In addition, the maximum UC duration is 28 weeks in Montana and 30 weeks in Massachusetts. When EB benefits are available, any available UC benefits above 26 weeks are treated effectively as if they were EB payments.

[3] 5 U.S.C. §8501-8508.

[4] 5 U.S.C. §8521-8525. For more information on the Unemployment Compensation for Ex-service members (UCX) program, see CRS Report RS22440, *Unemployment Compensation (Insurance) and Military Service*.

as other unemployed workers with respect to benefit levels, the waiting period for benefits, and benefit duration.

Although federal laws and regulations provide broad guidelines on UC benefit coverage, eligibility, and determination, the specifics regarding UC benefits are determined by each state.

This results in essentially 53 different programs.[5] UC eligibility is generally based on attaining qualified wages and employment in covered work over a 12-month period (called a base period) prior to unemployment. All states require a worker to have earned a certain amount of wages or to have worked for a certain period of time (or both) within the base period in order to be eligible to receive any UC benefits. The methods states use to determine eligibility vary greatly. Most state benefit formulas replace approximately half of a claimant's average weekly wage up to a weekly maximum.[6] In addition, each state's UC law requires individuals to have lost their jobs through no fault of their own and must be able to work, available for work, and actively seeking work. These eligibility requirements help ensure that UC benefits are directed toward workers with significant labor market experience who are unemployed because of economic conditions.

The UC program is financed by federal taxes under the Federal Unemployment Tax Act[7] (FUTA) and by state payroll taxes under the State Unemployment Tax Act (SUTA). The 0.6% effective net FUTA tax paid by employers on the first $7,000 of each employee's earnings (no more than $42 per worker per year) funds federal and state administrative costs, loans to insolvent state UC accounts, the federal share (50%) of EB payments, and state employment services.[8]

---

[5] The District of Columbia, Puerto Rico, and the Virgin Islands are considered to be states under UC law.

[6] For details on UC eligibility and benefits, see CRS Report RL33362, *Unemployment Insurance: Programs and Benefits*.

[7] 23 U.S.C. §§3301-11.

[8] The Federal Unemployment Tax Act (FUTA) imposes a 6.0% gross tax rate on the first $7,000 paid annually by employers to each employee. Employers in states with programs approved by the federal government and with no delinquent federal loans may credit 5.4 percentage points against the 6.0% tax rate, making the minimum net federal unemployment tax rate 0.6%. Details on how delinquent loans affect the net FUTA tax are in CRS Report RS22954, *The Unemployment Trust Fund (UTF): State Insolvency and Federal Loans to States*.

SUTA taxes on employers are limited by federal law to funding regular UC benefits and the state share (50%) of EB payments. Federal law requires that the state tax be on at least the first $7,000 of each employee's earnings (it may be more) and requires that the maximum state tax rate be at least 5.4%. Federal law also requires each employer's state tax rate to be based on the amount of UC paid to former employees (known as "experience rating"). Within these broad requirements, each state has great flexibility in determining its SUTA structure. Generally, the more UC benefits paid out to its former employees, the higher the tax rate of the employer, up to a maximum established by state law. Funds from FUTA and SUTA are deposited in the appropriate accounts within the Unemployment Trust Fund (UTF).

Extended Benefit Program

The EB program was established by the Federal-State Extended Unemployment Compensation Act of 1970 (EUCA; P.L. 91-373) (26 U.S.C. §3304, note). EUCA may extend receipt of unemployment benefits (extended benefits) at the state level if certain economic situations exist within the state. The President's FY2017 Budget Proposal contained several possible alternations to the EB program. See the "President's Budget Proposal for FY2017" section of this chapter for details on the proposals.

EB Triggers

The EB program is triggered when a state's insured unemployment rate (IUR) or total unemployment rate (TUR) reaches certain levels.[9] All states

[9] The total unemployment rate (TUR) is the three-month average of the ratio of unemployed workers to all workers (employed and unemployed) in the labor market. The TUR is essentially a three-month average version of the unemployment rate published by the Bureau of Labor Statistics (BLS) and based on data from the BLS's monthly Current Population Survey (CPS). The insured unemployment rate (IUR) is the ratio of UC claimants divided by individuals in UC-covered jobs. In addition, the IUR uses a different base of workers in its calculations as compared with the TUR. The IUR excludes several groups used in TUR calculations: self-employed workers, unpaid family workers, workers in certain not-for-profit organizations, and several other, primarily seasonal, categories of workers. In addition to those unemployed workers whose last jobs were in the excluded employment, the IUR

must pay up to 13 weeks of EB if the IUR for the previous 13 weeks is at least 5% and is 120% of the average of the rates for the same 13-week period in each of the two previous years. States may choose to enact two other optional thresholds. (States may choose one, two, or none.) If the state has chosen one or more of the EB trigger options, it would provide the following:

- Option 1—an additional 13 weeks of benefits if the state's IUR is at least 6%, regardless of previous years' averages.
- Option 2—an additional 13 weeks of benefits if the state's TUR is at least 6.5% and is at least 110% of the state's average TUR for the same 13 weeks in either of the previous two years; an additional 20 weeks of benefits if the state's TUR is at least 8% and is at least 110% of the state's average TUR for the same 13 weeks in either of the previous two years.

EB benefits are not "grandfathered" (phased out) when a state triggers "off" the program. When a state triggers "off" of an EB period, all EB benefit payments in the state cease immediately regardless of individual entitlement.[10]

The EB benefit amount is equal to the eligible individual's weekly regular UC benefits. Under permanent law, FUTA finances half (50%) of the EB payments and 100% of EB administrative costs.[11]

---

excludes the following: those who have exhausted their UC benefits (even if they are receiving EB benefits); new entrants or reentrants to the labor force; disqualified workers whose unemployment is considered to have resulted from their own actions rather than from economic conditions; and eligible unemployed persons who do not file for benefits.

[10] EB benefits on interstate claims are limited to two extra weeks unless *both* the worker's state of residence (e.g., Texas) and the worker's state of previous employment (e.g., Louisiana) are in an EB period.

[11] The Tax Relief, Unemployment Insurance Reauthorization, and Job Creation Act of 2010, P.L. 111-312, as amended (the final time by P.L. 112-240), made technical changes to certain triggers in the EB program. These changes allowed states to temporarily use lookback calculations based on three years of unemployment rate data (rather than the permanent-law lookback of two years of data) as part of their mandatory IUR and optional TUR triggers if states would otherwise trigger off or not be on a period of EB benefits. Using a two-year versus a three-year EB trigger lookback was an important adjustment at the time of the signing of P.L. 111-312 (December 17, 2010) because many states were likely to trigger off of their EB periods despite high, sustained—but not increasing—unemployment rates. For more

States fund the other half (50%) of EB benefit costs through their SUTA.[12]

Expired Emergency Unemployment Compensation Program

On June 30, 2008, President George W. Bush signed the Supplemental Appropriations Act of 2008 (P.L. 110-252), which created a new temporary unemployment insurance program, the EUC08 program. This was the eighth time Congress had created a federal temporary program to extend unemployment compensation during an economic slowdown.[13] State UC agencies administered the EUC08 benefit along with regular UC benefits.

The authorization for this program was extended multiple times since its enactment, but it was terminated on December 28, 2013, for all states except New York (December 29, 2013) and North Carolina (June 29, 2013).[14]

UNEMPLOYMENT INSURANCE BENEFITS AND THE SEQUESTER

The sequester order required by the Budget Control Act of 2011 (BCA; P.L. 112-25) and implemented on March 1, 2013 (after being delayed by P.L. 112-240), affected some but not all types of unemployment insurance

---

information on these state law changes, see CRS Report R41859, *Unemployment Insurance: Consequences of Changes in State Unemployment Compensation Laws*. The authorization for the temporary EB trigger modifications expired the week ending on or before December 31, 2013.

[12] P.L. 111-5, the American Recovery and Reinvestment Act of 2009 (most recently amended by P.L. 112-240, the American Taxpayer Relief Act of 2012), temporarily changed the federal-state funding arrangement for the EB program. The FUTA financed 100% of EB benefits from February 17, 2009, through December 31, 2013. The one exception to the 100% federal financing was for those "non-sharable" EB benefits (work not subject to FUTA taxes such as state and local government employment). Those non-sharable benefits continued to be 100% financed by the former employers.

[13] The other programs became effective in 1958, 1961, 1972, 1975, 1982, 1991, and 2002. For more details on these programs, see CRS Report RL34340, *Extending Unemployment Compensation Benefits During Recessions*.

[14] For more details on the early termination of EUC08 benefits in North Carolina, see CRS Report R41859, *Unemployment Insurance: Consequences of Changes in State Unemployment Compensation Laws*.

expenditures. Regular UC, UCX, and UCFE payments are not subject to the sequester reductions. EB, EUC08 (when available), and most forms of administrative funding are subject to the sequester reductions.[15]

FY2017 Sequester of UI Benefits

The FY2017 sequestration order required a 6.9% reduction in all nonexempt nondefense mandatory expenditures, but no sequestration reductions applicable to discretionary programs, projects, and activities.[16] Therefore, the sequestration order required that EB expenditures be reduced by 6.9% (only on the federal share of EB benefits) for weeks of unemployment beginning on October 8, 2016, through September 30, 2017. However, EB was not available in any state from the beginning of FY2017 through the time of this report date (April 2017).[17]

FY2016 Sequester of UI Benefits

Among many actions, the Bipartisan Budget Act of 2015, P.L. 114-74, increased discretionary spending limits for FY2016. As a result, although a 6.8% sequester reduction in non-exempt mandatory programs went into effect on October 1, 2015, for FY2016, there were nosequestration reductions applicable to discretionary programs, projects, and activities.[18]

---

[15] See CRS Report R42972, Sequestration as a Budget Enforcement Process: Frequently Asked Questions, for a discussion of the sequester order.

[16] Office of Management and Budget (OMB), OMB Report to the Congress on the Joint Committee Sequestration for Fiscal Year 2017, February 9, 2016, https://www.irs.gov/pub/whistleblower/2017_jc_sequestration_report_house.pdf.

[17] For details, see U.S. Department of Labor, Employment and Training Administration, *Unemployment Insurance Program Letter*, UIPL 9-17, January 19, 2017, https://wdr.doleta.gov/directives/attach/UIPL/UIPL_09-17_Acc.pdf.

[18] For details, see DOL, Employment and Training Administration, *Unemployment Insurance Program Letter*, UIPL 12-16, March 29, 2016, http://wdr.doleta.gov/directives/attach/UIPL/UIPL_12-16_Acc.pdf. For more information on the sequester order, see CRS Insight IN10389, *Bipartisan Budget Act of 2015: Adjustments to the Budget Control Act of 2011*.

However, if any EB benefits had become available, they would have been subject to the FY2016 6.8% sequestration reduction. Additionally, there may have been certain delayed EB or EUC08 benefit payments and related administrative costs made in FY2016 from prior fiscal years (for example, because of appeals). Those payments would have bene subject to the FY2016 6.8% sequestration reduction because FY2016 funds would have been apportioned for these purposes.

FY2015 Sequester of UI Benefits

In FY2015, the sequestration order required a 7.3% reduction in all nonexempt nondefense mandatory expenditures. Therefore, the sequestration order required that EB expenditures be reduced by 7.3% (only on the federal share of EB benefits) for weeks of unemployment beginning on October 4, 2014, through September 26, 2015. EB was not available in any state during FY2015.

State Fiscal Concerns Alleviating State Unemployment Compensation Stress

If a recession is deep enough and if state unemployment tax (SUTA) revenue is inadequate for long periods of time, states may have insufficient funds to pay for UC benefits. Federal law, which requires states to pay these benefits, provides a loan mechanism within the UTF framework that an insolvent state may opt to use to meet its UC benefit payment obligations.[19] States must pay back these loans. If the loans are not paid back quickly (depending on the timing of the beginning of the loan period), states may

[19] Federal UC law does not restrict the states from using loan resources outside of the UTF. Depending on state law, states may have other funding measures available and may be able to use funds from outside of the UTF to pay the benefits (such as issuing bonds).

face interest charges and the states' employers may face increased net FUTA rates until the loans are repaid.[20]

Near the end of the 114th Congress on October 18, 2016, only California and the Virgin Islands had outstanding loans. Together they owed a cumulative $3.6 billion to the federal accounts within the UTF.[21] In general, the increased state borrowing to fund UC benefits reflects the magnitude of the recession and the slow employment recovery afterward.[22]

President's Budget Proposal for FY2017

President Obama's budget proposal for FY2017 attempted to address some of the state and federal financing concerns.[23] In addition, the proposal would have expanded and reformed UI benefits and benefit availability.

Federal Unemployment Tax Changes

The President's budget proposal for FY2017 would have (1) reauthorized the lapsed 0.2% Federal Unemployment Tax (FUTA) surtax;[24]

---

[20] Details on how states may borrow federal funds to pay for UC benefits are in CRS Report RS22954, *The Unemployment Trust Fund (UTF): State Insolvency and Federal Loans to States*.

[21] For the most recent information on outstanding loans, see U.S. Department of the Treasury, Bureau of Public Debt, *Title XII Advance Activities Schedule* October 20, 2016, at http://www.treasurydirect.gov/govt/reports/tfmp/tfmp_advactivitiessched.htm.

[22] For the current solvency of each state's financing system, see DOL, Division of Fiscal and Actuarial Services, Office of Unemployment Insurance, *State Unemployment Insurance Trust Fund Solvency Report 2017*, March 2017, http://ows.doleta.gov/unemploy/docs/trust FundSolvReport.pdf.

[23] The President's detailed budget proposal for UC in FY2017 is accessible at http://www.dol.gov/sites/default/files/documents/general/budget/CBJ-2017-V1-08.pdf. For examples on previous proposals on changing the underlying tax structure, see reports released by the Advisory Council on Unemployment Compensation (ACUC), *Collected Findings and Recommendations: 1994-1996*, AUCU, Washington, DC, 1996. Additionally, the report proposed changes to the underlying loan requirements, some of which were incorporated into 20 C.F.R. §606.32 in 2010.

[24] Congress first passed a temporary FUTA surtax in 1976, and since 1983 the surtax had been applied as 0.2% on the first $7,000 of employee wages until it lapsed on July 1, 2011. Thus,

and (2) increased the taxable wage base to $40,000 while decreasing the effective FUTA tax rate to 0.165% (making it approximately actuarially equivalent to 0.8% on $7,000). After 2018, the taxable wage base would have been indexed to inflation. Beginning in 2018, the proposal would have required states to impose a minimum tax per employee that equates to 0.175% of the FUTA wage base ($70 per employee in 2018).

Requiring States to Maintain Increased UTF Balances

In addition, the President's budget proposal for FY2017 would have required states to maintain a UTF account balance of at least 50% of the state's Average High Cost Multiple (AHCM).[25] The proposal would have altered the rules for calculating the net FUTA rate, requiring a net FUTA rate on a state's employer if that state maintained an AHCM of less than 50% on two or more consecutive January firsts. The additional FUTA revenue would have been deposited into the state UTF account and would have been terminated once the AHCM met the 50% criteria.

State Requirement to Provide 26 Weeks of UC

The President's budget proposal for FY2017 would have required all states to have a maximum duration of at least 26 weeks for the regular UC program and adopt three policies that expand access to UC benefits. The states would have had to (1) enact an alternative base period option for determining UC eligibility; (2) not deny benefits for claimants who seek

---

since then, the effective FUTA tax on employers for each employee is 0.6% (a decrease from 0.8%) on the first $7,000 of wages.

[25] The average high-cost multiple (AHCM) is the ratio of actual UTF account balances to the average of the 3 highest years of benefit payments experienced by the state over the past 20 years. Presumably, the average of the 3 highest years' outlays would be a good indicator of potential expected UC payments if another recession were to occur. Under these assumptions, if a state had saved enough funds to pay for an average high year of UC benefit activity, its AHCM would be at least 1.0.

part-time employment; and (3) allow unemployed workers to be eligible for UI benefits if they leave their jobs for family reasons.[26]

Modernization Incentives

Finally, the President's budget proposal for FY2017 would have provided up to a total of $5 billion in lump sum payments to states for opting for changes that "modernize" state UC laws. To become eligible for the payments, states would have had to (1) provide for broader federal access to UI wage records; (2) adopt e-filing and/or increased penalties for employer non-reporting; (3) provide for at least 26 weeks of benefits in the regular UC program; and (4) define "misconduct" that conforms to the U.S. DOL model definition. States also would have had to commit to not make qualifying requirements more stringent or reduce benefit levels. Additionally, to receive the incentive payment, a state would have had to adopt two work incentive reforms and one benefit expansion reform.

The work incentive options would have included (1) progressively more intense reemployment service delivery as duration of benefit receipt lengthens; (2) improved reemployment services for UI claimants; (3) voluntary work-based programs for UI claimants, such as on-the-job training or apprenticeship programs or subsidized temporary work programs; (4) relocation assistance programs coupled with individual case management, in-person career counseling, provision of customized information on availability of job opportunities in other locations, and referrals to suitable

[26] The base period is the time period during which wages earned or hours/weeks worked are examined to determine a worker's monetary entitlement to UC. Almost all states use the first four of the last five completed calendar quarters preceding the filing of the claim as their base period. This may result in a lag of up to five months between the end of the base period and the date a worker becomes unemployed. As a result there are some instances when workers with substantial labor market attachment are ineligible for UC benefits. In particular, recent entrants to the workforce, or re- entrants, may be ineligible under this definition. Federal law allows states to develop expanded definitions of the base period. More than two-thirds of states allow the use of an alternative base period (ABP) for workers failing to qualify under the regular base period. For example, if the worker fails to qualify using wages and employment in the first four of the last five completed calendar quarters, then the state might use wages and employment in the last four completed calendar quarters.

jobs in other locations; and (5) improvement of data systems to enable and provide access to workforce and educational entities for performance, research, and evaluation.

The benefit expansion options would have included (1) allowing UC benefits to be paid to claimants in approved training; (2) establishing a maximum weekly benefit amount that is at least two-thirds of the state's average weekly wage in covered employment in the most recent 12- month period for which data are available; and (3) improving eligibility provisions related to temporary workers.

EB Reform

The President's budget proposal for FY2017 also would have altered and replaced most of the EB program. The mandatory IUR trigger would have been replaced by a modification of the current optional TUR trigger.[27] Funding for EB would have continued to be shared (50% state, 50% federal) if the maximum number of weeks of UC benefits available in the state was fewer than 26 weeks. Funding for EB would have been 100% reimbursed with federal funds if the state offered at least 26 weeks of UC. In addition, all EB claimants would have been required to receive Reemployment Services and Eligibility Assessments (RES/REAs) as a condition of eligibility.[28] If federal funds in the UTF were insufficient to pay EB, funds would have been

---

[27] The program would have had four tiers of 13 weeks each, using trigger thresholds of 6.5%, 7.5%, 8.5%, and 9.5%. This would have created up to 52 weeks of EB if a state met the economic conditions. A state could trigger onto a tier either by three-month average TUR at or above the percentage or by having an unemployment rate plus the change in rates from a comparable period in one of the previous two years at or above the trigger value.

[28] Reemployment and Eligibility Assessments (REAs) provide a means of enforcing job search requirements and delivering employment-related assistance to recipients. Since 2005, the federal government has provided grants to state workforce agencies to fund REAs. These are in-person interviews with selected UC claimants to assure that they are complying with the eligibility rules, determine if reemployment services are needed for the claimant to secure future employment, refer the individual to reemployment services (RES) as necessary, and provide labor market information that addresses the claimant's specific needs. REAs replaced a previous Eligibility Review Program that had been funded by DOL in which UC claimants were interviewed to confirm their eligibility for benefits. For more information, see the "Reemployment and Eligibility Assessments" section of CRS Report R43044, *Expediting the Return to Work: Approaches in the Unemployment Compensation Program*.

provided from the Treasury's General Fund through non-repayable advances.

Wage Insurance

The President's budget proposal for FY2017 would have created a new wage insurance[29] program that would have replaced half of lost wages, up to $10,000 over two years for certain formerly unemployed workers who find employment at lower salaries. The reemployed worker's new position would have had to pay less than $50,000/year and workers must have worked for their prior employer for at least three years to be eligible for this program.

ENACTED LAWS IN THE 114TH CONGRESS

The National Defense Authorization Act for Fiscal Year 2016 (P.L. 114-92)

Senator Ron Johnson sponsored S. 1356, which was enacted as the National Defense Authorization Act for Fiscal Year 2016, P.L. 114-92. In addition to many other actions, the law altered certain conditions for individuals to receive Unemployment Compensation for Former Service members (UCX).[30] The law generally prohibits the concurrent receipt of UCX and Post-9/11 Veterans Educational Assistance but does provide exceptions.[31] In addition, the law doubled the number of days (from 90 to

---

[29] For information on Wage Insurance and UC, see CRS Report R43044, Expediting the Return to Work: Approaches in the Unemployment Compensation Program.

[30] For information on UCX, see CRS Report RS22440, *Unemployment Compensation (Insurance) and Military Service*. For information on Post-9/11 Veterans Educational Assistance see CRS Report R42755, *The Post-9/11 Veterans' Educational Assistance Act of 2008 (Post-9/11 GI Bill): A Primer*.

[31] 5 U.S.C. §8525(a) provides exceptions to the prohibition on concurrent receipt of UCX and educational assistance.

180 continuous days) a reserve member of the Armed Forces would have to be on active duty to qualify for UCX.

Two earlier proposals had similar provisions, but did not include exceptions to the prohibition of concurrent receipt. Representative Mac Thornberry sponsored H.R. 1735, the National Defense Authorization Act for Fiscal Year 2016,[32] which was vetoed by President Obama on October 22, 2015. Senator John McCain sponsored an identically named bill (S. 1376) that contained similar provisions.

LEGISLATIVE PROPOSALS IN THE 114TH CONGRESS

Concurrent Receipt of SSDI and UI Benefits[33]

S. 499 (Senator Orin Hatch), S. 2005 (Senator David Vitter), and H.R. 918 (Representative Sam Johnson), all titled the Social Security Disability Insurance and Unemployment Benefits Double Dip Elimination Act, would have required for any month that an individual is entitled to UC, EB, or Trade Adjustment Assistance (TAA) for at least one week, he or she would have been deemed to have engaged in substantial gainful activity (SGA) and be disqualified from receiving SSDI benefits. If an SSDI beneficiary had been participating in a period of trial work, the individual would have been deemed to have rendered services in a month if he or she had been entitled to UC, EB, or TAA for any week that month (and, therefore, that month would count toward the 60- month rolling period in the trial work period without having the benefits reduced or terminated).

---

[32] The bill contained two provisions regarding unemployment insurance for former service members. Section 535 of S. 1376 included a provision that would have prohibited the concurrent receipt of unemployment benefits for former military service members (UCX) and Post-9/11 Veterans Educational Assistance. Section 592 of the bill would have doubled the number of days a reserve member of the armed forces would have to be on active duty to qualify for UCX (from 90 to 180).

[33] For an overview of concurrent receipt of SSDI and UI benefits in the 114th Congress, see CRS Report R43471, Concurrent Receipt of Social Security Disability Insurance (SSDI) and Unemployment Insurance (UI): Background and Legislative Proposals.

H.R. 5919, the Preserving and Reforming SSDI (PAR-SSDI) Act of 2016, was introduced by Representative David Schweikert. H.R. 5919 would have required (among other provisions) that for any week in whole or in part within a month that an individual was paid or determined to be eligible for UC, he or she would have been deemed to have engaged in substantial gainful activity and so be disqualified from receiving Social Security disability benefits after a certain period has elapsed.

S. 343, the Reducing Overlapping Payments Act, was introduced by Senator Jeff Flake. S. 343 would have required for any month that an individual was entitled to UC, no SSDI benefits would be paid.

UI Program Integrity

Representative David Reichert sponsored H.R. 2503, the Permanently Ending Receipt by Prisoners Act. H.R. 2503 would have required states to use the Prisoner Update Processing System (PUPS) data compiled by the Social Security Administration.[34] States would use PUPS data to confirm that an individual was not confined in a jail, prison, or other penal institution or correctional facility. Any individual who was incarcerated would not be eligible for regular UC benefits because the individual would not have been available for work.

Representative Kevin Brady sponsored H.R. 2512, the Furloughed Federal Employee Double Dip Elimination Act. The bill would have clarified that if a federal employee were to receive back pay for a period during which he or she had been furloughed due to a lapse in federal appropriations, the federal employee would have to repay any unemployment compensation for that period.

---

[34] The Prisoner Update Processing System (PUPS) data contain the individual's name, Social Security number, date of birth, sex, date of conviction, date of confinement, release date, inmate status code, and such other information as may be supplied or acquired during the benefit suspension or reinstatement process.

Drug Testing[35]

Representative Steve Pearce sponsored H.R. 1136, the Accountability in Unemployment Act of 2015. The bill would have required individuals to undergo drug testing and test negative to be eligible for UC benefits. H.R. 1136 would also have required a 30-day waiting period for applicants who test positive for any one of several specified drugs and would have required individuals to be ineligible for UC benefits for five years after the third positive drug test.

Representative Earl Carter sponsored H.R. 2148, the Ensuring Quality in the Unemployment Insurance Program (EQUIP) Act. The bill would have required any UC applicant to complete a substance abuse risk assessment. If the applicant had been deemed high-risk, the applicant would have to pass a controlled substances test to receive UC benefits. Those who did not pass the test would be ineligible for benefits for 30 days and then would have to be retested to determine eligibility.

Representative Kevin Brady introduced H.R. 5945, the Ready to Work Act of 2016. The proposal would have terminated the final rule issued by the U.S. DOL on August 1, 2016, the "Federal-State Unemployment Compensation Program; Middle Class Tax Relief and Job Creation Act of 2012 Provision on Establishing Appropriate Occupations for Drug Testing of Unemployment Compensation Applicants" (81 Fed. Reg. 50298). This DOL rule established occupations that regularly conduct drug testing. As such, the rule implemented a change made under the Middle Class Tax Relief and Job Creation Act of 2012 (P.L. 112-96; February 22, 2012) that allowed states to drug test UC applicants for whom suitable work is available only in an occupation that regularly conducts drug testing.

---

[35] For implications of required drug testing, see CRS Report R42326, *Constitutional Analysis of Suspicionless Drug Testing Requirements for the Receipt of Governmental Benefits*.

Rehiring UI Beneficiaries and Exhaustees

Representative Bill Pascrell introduced H.R. 481, the Long-Term Unemployed Hiring Incentive Act. The bill would have extended the work opportunity tax credit (WOTC) for companies that hire any UC exhaustees through December 31, 2017.[36]

Representative Julia Brownley introduced H.R. 2265, the VOW to Hire Heroes Extension Act of 2015, and Senator Richard Blumenthal introduced an identically named bill, S. 1517. This legislation would have expanded and extended WOTC for companies that hire veterans through December 31, 2018. In addition, the bill would have expanded the program by allowing tax-exempt organizations to apply a credit against payroll taxes for hiring a veteran.

Representative Barbara Lee introduced H.R. 2721, the Pathways Out of Poverty Act of 2015, and Representative Frederica Wilson introduced H.R. 3555. Both proposals would have amended the work opportunity tax credit to allow an increased work opportunity tax credit for long-term unemployed individuals (individuals who are unemployed and receiving unemployment compensation for six months or more).

Representative David McKinley introduced the Manufacturing Economic Recovery Act of 2015, H.R. 3622. The bill, among other items, would have created a permanent work opportunity tax credit for hiring a full-time employee in a manufacturing facility located in the United States and included an increased credit for hiring individuals receiving unemployment compensation.

Delegate Eleanor Holmes Norton introduced the Reducing Long-Term Unemployment Act, H.R. 4593. The bill would have suspended employment and railroad retirement taxes for employers who hired unemployed individuals through 2017. The aggregate reduction in taxes from such suspension would have been limited to $5,000 per employee.

---

[36] The authorization of the WOTC was extended after the introduction of this proposal by P.L. 114-113. Under current law, wages earned by eligible workers who begin work before December 31, 2019, are eligible for the WOTC. For additional information on WOTC, see CRS Report R43729, *The Work Opportunity Tax Credit*.

Representative Bonnie Watson Coleman introduced the Investing in Older Americans Act of 2016, H.R. 4973. The bill would have made the WOTC permanent and expanded it to include the hiring of older long-term unemployment recipients who are at least 55 years old at the time of hiring. The bill would have limited the amount of the qualified first-year wages that may be taken into account under the WOTC to $14,000 for a qualified older long-term unemployment recipient.

Reauthorize Emergency Unemployment Compensation

Two bills would have reauthorized the lapsed temporary Emergency Unemployment Compensation (EUC08) benefits until the end of 2015: H.R. 2721, the Pathways Out of Poverty Act of 2015 and H.R. 3555, the Jobs! Jobs! Jobs! Act of 2015 (Representative Frederica Wilson).

Vouchers and Demonstration Projects

Representative James Renacci sponsored H.R. 2509, the Flexibility to Promote Reemployment Act. The bill would have made a number of changes to the state UC demonstration projects created by the Middle Class Tax Relief and Job Creation Act of 2012 (P.L. 112-96).[37] The bill would have extended the time period that the (now-expired) state demonstration projects could be approved by DOL through December 31, 2019 (P.L. 112-96 authorized these demonstration projects through December 31, 2015), as well as expanded the existing authority for state UC demonstration projects by authorizing 10 states per year to conduct approved demonstration projects (the original, expired authority was only for 10 states total). H.R. 2509 also would have revised state UC demonstration project requirements, including removing a requirement that any direct disbursements paid to employers for

---

[37] For more details on these state UC demonstration projects, as authorized under 42 U.S.C. §505, see CRS Report R41662, *Unemployment Insurance: Legislative Issues in the 112th Congress*.

hiring UC claimants not exceed an individual's UC weekly benefit amount and requiring that DOL approve state applications for UC demonstration projects based on the order of receipt. Additionally, the bill would have transferred the responsibility for the state UC demonstration project impact evaluation from the states, as under the now-expired demonstration authority, to DOL and would have required a specific procedure for termination of the state UC demonstration project by DOL.

Both H.R. 2721, the Pathways Out of Poverty Act of 2015, and H.R. 3555, the Jobs! Jobs! Jobs! Act of 2015, among many provisions, would have allowed states to (1) establish a Bridge to Work program to provide EUC08 claimants with short-term work experience placements with eligible employers; (2) provide a wage insurance program to pay, for up to two years, an EUC08 claimant who obtains reemployment up to 50% of the difference between the wages received at the time of work separation and the wages received for reemployment; and (3) provide a program of enhanced reemployment services to EUC08 claimants, including unemployed individuals who have exhausted their EUC08 rights.

Job Training and Education

Representative Rodney Davis sponsored H.R. 2219, the Opportunity KNOCKs Act. The bill would have required that states allow UC beneficiaries to participate in a Workforce Investment Act (WIA) authorized job training program and remain eligible for benefits.[38] If the UC beneficiary has been profiled to exhaust regular benefits, the individual would have been allowed to enroll in any coursework necessary to attain a recognized postsecondary credential.

---

[38] The Workforce Innovation and Opportunity Act of 2014 (WIOA; P.L. 113-128) amended and reauthorized many Workforce Investment Act (WIA) programs.

Relocation Subsidies

Representative Tony Cárdenas sponsored H.R. 2755, the American Worker Mobility Act of 2015. The proposal would have authorized the U.S. Department of Labor to grant a relocation subsidy of up to $10,000 to long-term unemployed workers.

Short-Time Compensation[39]

Both H.R. 2721, the Pathways Out of Poverty Act of 2015, and H.R. 3555, the Jobs! Jobs! Jobs! Act of 2015, would have provided temporary 100% federal financing for up to three years and six months after enactment for short-time compensation (STC) benefits in states with existing STC programs. States without existing STC programs would have been allowed to enter into an agreement with DOL for up to two years and three months after enactment and receive federal reimbursement for administrative expenses, as well as temporary federal financing of 50% of STC payments to individuals, with employers paying the other 50% of STC costs. If a state would have entered into an agreement with the Secretary of Labor and then subsequently enacted a law providing for STC, that state would have been eligible to receive 100% federal financing at that enactment.

The proposals would have awarded grants of up to $700 million total to eligible states, with one-third of each state's grant available for implementation and improved administration purposes and two-thirds of each state's grant available for program promotion and enrollment of employers. This proposal would have provided $1.5 million for DOL to submit a report to Congress and the President, within four years of enactment, on the implementation of this provision.

Representative Rosa DeLauro and Senator Jack Reed introduced the Layoff Prevention Extension Act of 2016, H.R. 5408 and S. 1902, respectively. The proposals would have extended federal financing of the

---

[39] See CRS Report R40689, Compensated Work Sharing Arrangements (Short-Time Compensation) as an Alternative to Layoffs, for details on STC.

STC programs for an additional two years. Additionally, they would have extended the deadline by two years for a state to submit its application for a STC grant through December 31, 2016.

Unemployment Benefits for Energy Workers

Senator Bernie Sanders introduced S. 2398, the Clean Energy Worker Just Transition Act. Among other provisions, the proposal would have provided additional weeks of unemployment benefits for adversely affected workers in coal-related or coal-dependent or similar energy industries. The workers' employment status would have had to change for causes attributable to the low cost of competing alternative forms of energy.[40]

Representative Evan Jenkins introduced H.R. 5669, the Creating Opportunities for America's Laid-off (COAL) Miners Act of 2016. The proposal would have added up to 26 weeks of additional unemployment benefits for adversely affected workers in coal-related or coal-dependent or similar energy industries.

Domestic Violence

Representative Lucille Roybal-Allard and Senator Patty Murray introduced the Security and Financial Empowerment Act of 2015, H.R. 3841 and S. 2208, respectively. The bills would have required states to consider an individual who quit a job as a result of domestic or sexual violence to be eligible for UC benefits.

---

[40] The assistance would have included temporary additional unemployment compensation, health insurance premium subsidy tax credits, training and support for employment, as well as additional pension benefits.

In: Unemployment Insurance
Editor: Arlette Bolk
ISBN: 978-1-53614-937-1

Chapter 4

UNEMPLOYMENT AND EMPLOYMENT PROGRAMS AVAILABLE TO WORKERS AFFECTED BY DISASTERS*

Benjamin Collins, David H. Bradley, Katelin P. Isaacs and Julie M. Whittaker

SUMMARY

The federal government supports several programs that can provide assistance to workers who lose their jobs as a result of a natural or other disaster. In many cases, disaster-affected workers will be served by permanent programs and systems that generally provide assistance to workers who involuntarily lose their jobs. In some cases, disaster-triggered federal supports may be made available to provide additional assistance or aid to workers who do not qualify for assistance under the permanent programs.

This chapter discusses two income support programs and two workforce service programs. In each benefit category, there is a broader permanent program and a more-targeted program for disaster-affected

* This is an edited, reformatted and augmented version of Congressional Research Service, Publication No. R45182, dated April 30, 2018.

workers. All of these programs are administered through state agencies and some programmatic details may be state-specific.

- Unemployment Compensation (UC) provides a weekly cash payment to workers who are involuntarily unemployed and meet other criteria. States administer UC benefits with U.S. Department of Labor (DOL) oversight. UC benefits are considered entitlements for eligible workers and funded via payroll taxes paid by employers.
- Disaster Unemployment Assistance (DUA) provides a weekly cash payment to individuals who become unemployed as a direct result of a major disaster and are not eligible for UC benefits. DUA is funded by the federal government and benefits are paid through each state's UC agency.
- Dislocated Worker Activities under the Workforce Innovation and Opportunity Act (WIOA-DW) are federal formula grants to states to provide training and career services to workers who involuntarily lose their jobs and meet other criteria. WIOA-DW grants are funded via DOL appropriations and administered by state workforce agencies and local partners with DOL oversight.
- Disaster Dislocated Worker Grants (DDWGs) are competitive federal grants that support temporary disaster response jobs for workers who are unemployed as a direct result of a disaster. DDWGs are awarded by DOL to the state and local partners that receive WIOA-DW funds.

Since UC and DUA outlays increase as the need grows, these funds can be responsive to the scale of a disaster. Conversely, WIOA-DW and DDWG funds are limited by appropriations levels and therefore may be less immediately scalable than UC and DUA, which are entitlements for individuals.

In some instances, Congress has enacted legislation to temporarily expand these programs that serve disaster-affected workers or otherwise extend supplemental support to the states administering them. These prior efforts may serve as a model when Congress considers legislation to support workers affected by disasters.

INTRODUCTION

Workers who lose their jobs due to a natural or other disaster can seek assistance through several federally supported programs. In many cases, disaster-affected workers will be served by permanent programs and systems that provide assistance to workers who involuntarily lose their jobs. In some cases, entities located within geographic areas affected by disasters can qualify for additional support that is limited to serving disaster-affected workers.

This chapter discusses two income support programs and two employment service programs. In each benefit category, there is a broader permanent program and a more-targeted program for disaster-affected workers.

- Unemployment Compensation[1] (UC) provides a weekly cash payment to workers who are involuntarily unemployed and meet other criteria. States administer UC benefits with U.S. Department of Labor (DOL) oversight. UC is financed via payroll taxes paid by employers: UC benefits are funded by state unemployment taxes (SUTA) and UC administration is funded by a federal unemployment tax (FUTA). UC benefits are considered entitlements for eligible workers and are required to be paid promptly.
- Disaster Unemployment Assistance (DUA) provides a weekly cash payment to individuals who become unemployed as a direct result of a major disaster and are not eligible for UC benefits. DUA is funded through the Federal Emergency Management Agency (FEMA) and administered by DOL through each state's UC agency.
- Dislocated Worker Activities under the Workforce Innovation and Opportunity Act (WIOA-DW) provides federal formula grants to states to provide training and career services to workers who involuntarily lose their jobs and meet other criteria. WIOA-DW grants are funded via discretionary appropriations to DOL and administered by state workforce agencies and local partners with DOL oversight.
- Disaster Dislocated Worker Grants (DDWGs) provide competitive federal grants that support temporary disaster response jobs for workers who are unemployed as a direct result of a disaster.

[1] Unemployment Compensation is often referred to as Unemployment Insurance (UI).

DDWGs are awarded by DOL to the state and local partners that receive WIOA-DW funds.

In terms of scale, the primary infusion of funds for disaster-affected workers will typically come from increased numbers of UC payments and, to a lesser extent, the availability of DUA benefits. Because UC and DUA outlays increase as the need grows, these funds can be responsive to the scale of a disaster. Conversely, WIOA-DW and DDWG funds are typically limited by annual appropriations and therefore may be less scalable than UC and DUA, which are entitlements for individuals.

This chapter focuses on programs that provide assistance to workers on the basis of job loss due to a disaster. Other programs that may support such disaster-affected individuals but do not have job loss as an eligibility criterion are not included.[2] Similarly, this chapter does not discuss programs that may assist workers who lost their jobs due to a disaster but establish eligibility based on criteria other than job loss, such as being low-income.[3]

ROLE OF DISASTER DECLARATIONS IN BENEFIT RECEIPT

Since some of the systems that support disaster-affected workers are permanent and have general eligibility criteria, benefit receipt is not contingent on a disaster meeting specific criteria. For example, disaster-affected workers may qualify for UC on the basis of becoming unemployed due to conditions created by a disaster (e.g., the place of business is closed because of a disaster), but benefit receipt does not require the presence of a specific type or magnitude of disaster. Similarly, the WIOA-DW system serves workers whose job loss is due to a disaster as well as workers who lose their jobs for other reasons.

---

[2] For a broader discussion of federal resources available to disaster-affected individuals, see CRS Report RL31734, *Federal Disaster Assistance Response and Recovery Programs: Brief Summaries*.

[3] For example, many programs establish eligibility based on income. For a discussion of more general low-income programs, see CRS Report R44574, *Federal Benefits and Services for People with Low Income: Overview of Spending Trends, FY2008-FY2015*.

DUA and DDWG are contingent on disasters being declared as such.[4] DUA benefits are available only to those individuals who have become unemployed as a direct result of a declared major disaster as determined under the Robert T. Stafford Disaster Relief and Emergency Assistance Act (P.L. 100-707, the Stafford Act) and if the disaster declaration includes the notice of availability of DUA benefits.[5] DDWG assistance can be awarded in response to a disaster or emergency declared under the Stafford Act or "an emergency or disaster situation of national significance that could result in a potentially large loss of employment, as declared or otherwise recognized ... by a federal agency."[6]

Benefit Access through State and Local Providers

The benefits described in this chapter are administered through state workforce systems and state unemployment compensation agencies. The specific processes for accessing benefits will vary by state. Workers can access state-specific information via the Department of Labor's Career One Stop website at http://www.careeronestop.org/.

Income Support: Benefits from Unemployment Insurance Programs

The joint federal-state UC program is permanently authorized and provides income support through weekly UC benefit payments to eligible unemployed workers. The DUA program provides income support to individuals who become unemployed as a direct result of a major disaster

[4] For a description of the FEMA disaster declaration process, see CRS Report R43784, *FEMA's Disaster Declaration Process: A Primer*.

[5] The Stafford Act authorizes the President to issue a major disaster declaration after state and local government resources have been overwhelmed by a natural catastrophe or "regardless of cause, any fire, flood, or explosion in any part of the United States."

[6] See 29 U.S.C. 3225(a)(1). DOL notes that "Federal declarations from the Department of Commerce and the Small Business Administration are examples of eligible federal declarations." See https://www.doleta.gov/DWGs/Types-ofDWGs/Disaster-Emergency-DWGs/.

and are not eligible for UC benefits. These unemployment insurance programs are entitlement programs funded through direct spending; benefits provided through these programs are not limited by appropriations. Consequently, these programs may be responsive to unemployment caused by disasters.

Unemployment Compensation[7]

Created under the Social Security Act of 1935, UC is a joint federal-state system that provides unemployment benefits to eligible individuals who become involuntarily unemployed for economic reasons and meet state-established eligibility rules.

Financing and Administration

States administer UC benefits with oversight from DOL. Although federal laws and regulations provide some broad guidelines on UC benefit coverage, eligibility, and benefit determination, the specifics of benefits are determined by each state. This results in essentially 53 different UC programs.[8]

The UC program is financed by federal payroll taxes (FUTA) and state payroll taxes (SUTA). The 0.6% effective net FUTA tax paid by employers on the first $7,000 of each employee's earnings (no more than $42 per worker per year) funds federal and state administrative costs, loans to insolvent state UC accounts, the federal share (50%) of Extended Benefit (EB) payments, and state employment services. States levy their own payroll taxes (SUTA taxes) on employers to fund regular UC benefits and the state share of the EB program. SUTA is "experience rated" in all states; that is, the SUTA rate is based on the amount of UC paid to former employees. Generally, the more UC benefits paid to its former employees, the higher the

---

[7] For additional details on UC, see CRS Report RL33362, *Unemployment Insurance: Programs and Benefits*.

[8] The District of Columbia, Puerto Rico, and the Virgin Islands are considered to be states under UC law.

tax rate of the employer, up to a maximum established by state law. The experience rating is intended to ensure an equitable distribution of UC program taxes among employers in relation to their use of the UC program, and to encourage a stable workforce.[9]

If economic conditions, such as recession, require the payment of UC benefits such that SUTA revenue is inadequate, states may have insufficient funds to pay for their UC benefits. Federal law, which requires states to pay these benefits, provides a loan mechanism within the Unemployment Trust Fund (UTF) framework that an insolvent state may opt to use to meet its UC benefit payment obligations. States must pay back these loans. If the loans are not paid back quickly (depending on the timing of the beginning of the loan period), states may face interest charges and the states' employers may face increased net FUTA rates until the loans are repaid.[10]

Individual Eligibility

The UC program pays benefits to workers who become involuntarily unemployed for economic reasons and meet state-established eligibility rules. The UC program generally does not provide UC benefits to the self-employed, those who are unable to work, or those who do not have a recent earnings history. Additionally, states usually disqualify claimants who lost their jobs because of inability to work, voluntarily quit without good cause, were discharged for job-related misconduct, or refused suitable work without good cause. In order to receive UC benefits, claimants must have enough recent earnings (distributed over a specified period) to meet their state's earnings requirements; and be able to, available for, and actively searching for work.

---

[9] For additional details on UC financing, see CRS Report R44527, Unemployment Compensation: The Fundamentals of the Federal Unemployment Tax (FUTA); and CRS Report RS22077, Unemployment Compensation (UC) and the Unemployment Trust Fund (UTF): Funding UC Benefits.

[10] For additional details on federal loans to states to pay UC benefits, see CRS Report RS22954, *The Unemployment Trust Fund (UTF): State Insolvency and Federal Loans to States.*

Supported Services and Benefits

The UC program provides income support to eligible workers through the payment of weekly cash benefits during a spell of unemployment. UC benefits are available for a maximum duration of up to 26 weeks in most states.[11]

UC benefits may be extended at the state level by the permanent law Extended Benefits (EB) program if high unemployment exists within the state. After regular unemployment benefits are exhausted, the EB program may provide up to an additional 13 or 20 weeks of benefits, depending on worker eligibility, state law, and economic conditions in the state. The EB program was established by the Federal-State Extended Unemployment Compensation Act of 1970 (EUCA; P.L. 91-373).[12]

Disaster-Related Considerations

Workers who become unemployed as a result of a disaster may qualify for UC. For example, if a natural disaster damages a place of employment and the condition of the facility prevents the employees from working, the displaced workers may qualify for UC if they meet all the eligibility requirements.

The UC program generally does not provide benefits to the self-employed, individuals who are unable to work, or individuals who do not have a recent earnings history. However, when a major disaster is declared, victims who would typically be ineligible for UC may be eligible for DUA.

In cases where a disaster creates increased unemployment, a state may be more likely to meet the criteria to trigger onto an EB period and, thus, provide EB benefits to eligible individuals in that state.[13]

---

[11] For details on states with less than 26 weeks of UC available, see CRS Report R41859, *Unemployment Insurance: Consequences of Changes in State Unemployment Compensation Laws*.

[12] See 26 U.S.C. §3304, note.

[13] For example, due to increased unemployment rates in the aftermath of Hurricanes Irma and Maria, the Virgin Islands triggered onto an EB period that began December 17, 2017; therefore, an additional 13 weeks of EB benefits (in addition to UC benefits of up to 26 weeks) became available in the Virgin Islands.

Disaster Unemployment Assistance[14]

The DUA program provides income support to individuals who become unemployed as a direct result of a major disaster and are not eligible for UC benefits. First created in 1970 through P.L. 91-606, DUA benefits are authorized by the Stafford Act.[15]

Financing and Administration

DUA benefits are funded through the Disaster Relief Fund (DRF) administered by the Federal Emergency Management Agency (FEMA). The DRF is funded annually through appropriations and is a "no-year" account, meaning that any unused funds from the previous fiscal year (if available) are carried over to the next fiscal year. In general, when the balance of the DRF becomes low, Congress provides additional funding through both annual and supplemental appropriations to replenish the account.[16] DOL administers the DUA program and coordinates with FEMA to provide the funds to the state UC agencies for payment of DUA benefits and payment of state administration costs under agreements with DOL.

Qualifying Events

Based on the request of the affected state's governor, the President may declare a major disaster. The declaration identifies the areas in the state eligible for assistance. The declaration of a major disaster provides the full range of disaster assistance available under the Stafford Act, which may include, but is not limited to, the repair, replacement, or reconstruction of public and nonprofit facilities; cash grants for the personal needs of victims; housing; and unemployment assistance related to job loss from the disaster (i.e., DUA).

---

[14] For more information on DUA, see CRS Report RS22022, *Disaster Unemployment Assistance (DUA)*.

[15] See 42 U.S.C. 5122(2). Authorization for DUA can be found in the Stafford Act, Section 410, P.L. 100-707, 42 U.S.C. 5177. Regulations can be found at 20 C.F.R. 625.

[16] For details of DRF funding see CRS Report R43537, *FEMA's Disaster Relief Fund: Overview and Selected Issues*.

Individual Eligibility

Disaster-affected workers who are ineligible for UC may be eligible for DUA. The DUA benefits are available only to those individuals who work or live in the area of a declared disaster and have become unemployed as a direct result of the disaster.

The individual eligibility requirements for DUA differ significantly from the UC program requirements. For example, eligibility for DUA benefits does not necessarily require that the individual have a substantial work history, and in some cases does not require that the worker be available for work (unlike the UC program requirements). In particular, the DUA regulation defines eligible unemployed workers to include

- the self-employed,
- workers who experience a "week of unemployment" following the date the major disaster began when such unemployment is a direct result of the major disaster,
- workers unable to reach the place of employment as a direct result of the major disaster,
- workers who were to begin employment and do not have a job or are unable to reach the job as a direct result of the major disaster,
- individuals who have become the breadwinner or major provider of support for a household because the head of the household has died as a direct result of the major disaster,[17] and
- workers who cannot work because of injuries caused as a direct result of the major disaster.

As with state UC programs, workers who do not have permission to work legally in the United States are not eligible for DUA benefits. Noncitizens must have a Social Security number and an alien registration card number in order to apply for DUA benefits.

---

[17] The survivor who becomes the head of household is not required to have wage credits and could be eligible for DUA independently of whether the deceased household head would have been eligible for UC benefits.

Generally, applications must be filed within 30 days after the date the state announces availability of DUA benefits. When applicants have good cause, they may file claims after the 30-day deadline. This deadline may be extended. However, initial applications filed after the 26th week following the declaration date are not considered.

Because DUA beneficiaries are not entitled to regular UC benefits, they are not eligible to receive Extended Benefits (EB).

Supported Services and Benefits

DUA benefits are generally calculated by state UC agencies under the provisions of the state law for UC in the state where the disaster occurred. When a reasonable comparative earnings history can be constructed, DUA benefits are determined in a similar manner to regular state UC benefit rules. Self-employed persons are expected to bring in their tax records to prove a level of earnings for the previous two years. These records would take the place of the employer-reported wage data in UC benefit determination. Likewise, workers who would otherwise be eligible for UC benefits except for the injuries caused as a direct result of the disaster that make them unavailable for work would receive DUA benefits in an amount equivalent to what they would have received under the UC system if they were available to work.

Workers who do not have an employment history sufficient to qualify for UC benefits (either as a new worker or recent hire) receive a DUA benefit equivalent to half of the average UC benefit for their state. The maximum weekly benefit amount is determined under the provisions of the state law and cannot be more than the maximum UC benefit available in that state. The minimum weekly DUA benefit a worker may receive is half of the average weekly UC benefit for the state where the disaster occurred.

EMPLOYMENT SERVICES: DISLOCATED WORKER PROGRAMS

Two related programs for dislocated workers can assist individuals who involuntarily lose their jobs due to a disaster. Federally funded Dislocated Worker Activities grants under the Workforce Innovation and Opportunity Act (WIOA, P.L. 113-128) are formula grants to states to provide job training and career services to individuals who lose their jobs, while Disaster Dislocated Worker Grants are competitive grants that support the provision of temporary jobs for workers who become unemployed as a result of a disaster.

WIOA Dislocated Worker Activities[18]

WIOA authorizes formula grants to state workforce agencies to support dislocated workers.[19] The bulk of a state's WIOA Dislocated Worker (WIOA-DW) funds are subgranted to local workforce development boards that provide actual workforce services. WIOA-DW funds may support career services or training benefits for qualified workers, including workers who become unemployed as a result of a disaster.

Financing and Administration

WIOA-DW funds are funded by discretionary appropriations. Statute specifies that 20% of WIOA-DW funds are allotted to a national reserve that primarily supports National Dislocated Worker Grants (including Disaster Dislocated Worker Grants, described later in this chapter). The unreserved

---

[18] For more information on WIOA Dislocated Worker Activities and other programs authorized by WIOA, see CRS Report R44252, *The Workforce Innovation and Opportunity Act and the One-Stop Delivery System.*

[19] For the purposes of this program, Puerto Rico is considered a state. While not eligible as states, American Samoa, Guam, the Northern Mariana Islands, Palau, and the U.S. Virgin Islands also may qualify for WIOA-DW funding.

funds are allotted to state workforce agencies via a formula that considers several unemployment-related factors.[20]

From the WIOA-DW funds that are allotted to the states, governors may reserve up to 15% for statewide activities ("governor's reserve") and up to 25% for rapid response activities that respond to large-scale layoffs. The remainder of the state's WIOA-DW grant is allocated to local workforce development boards that provide or facilitate services and benefits to individual workers.

Individual Eligibility

Generally, an eligible dislocated worker for the purposes of this program is a worker who (1) has involuntarily lost his or her job, (2) has demonstrated a labor force attachment, typically through eligibility for UC, and (3) is unlikely to return to his or her prior job.[21] Workers whose job loss is attributable to a disaster and who meet the other criteria for dislocated workers may access services supported by WIOA-DW grants.

In cases where funding is insufficient to serve all eligible dislocated workers, statute specifies that local providers must prioritize low-income individuals. The WIOA definition of low-income includes recipients of certain means-tested benefits as well as homeless individuals.[22]

Supported Services and Benefits

Services under WIOA-DW are separated into career services and training. Career services can include assessment of skills and needs, provision of labor market information, and various forms of job search assistance. Training is provided through individual training accounts and can include occupational classroom training, on-the-job training, or more general job readiness training.[23] Local providers have a great deal of

---

[20] Formula funds are allocated on the basis of each state's relative share of (1) unemployment, (2) excess unemployment, and (3) long-term unemployment. The full formula is specified at WIOA, Section 132(b)(2)(B); 29 U.S.C. 3172.

[21] For full definition, see Section 3(15) of WIOA; 29 U.S.C. 3102(15).

[22] For full criteria, see Section 3(36) of WIOA; 29 U.S.C. 3102(36).

[23] For more information on allowable uses of grant funds, see Section 134 of WIOA; 29 U.S.C. 3174.

discretion in the specific career services and training benefits that are provided to each eligible dislocated worker.

Disaster-Related Considerations

A worker who loses his or her job due to a disaster may not qualify for WIOA-DW services if he or she does not meet other dislocated worker criteria in law. For example, if a worker displaced by a disaster is expected to return to his or her prior job, the worker would not qualify. Disaster-affected workers who do not meet WIOA-DW eligibility criteria may seek assistance under less-targeted WIOA funding streams (see subsequent "WIOA Adult Activities" section).

The governor's reserve is designed to allow the state to respond to unanticipated mass layoffs, such as layoffs due to a disaster (natural or otherwise). The governor may use funds from the reserve to support "rapid response" activities in areas within the state that experience large-scale dislocation. These rapid response activities include contacting dislocated workers immediately after dislocation to determine eligibility for various benefits and services as well as developing a coordinated local response in seeking state economic development aid.

The WIOA-DW formula does not specifically target funds to disaster-affected areas. Because the formula is based on unemployment factors, areas with high levels of unemployment after a disaster may qualify for higher levels of funding in subsequent years' formula allocations. Due to the construction and implementation of the formula, however, it is possible that unemployment that results from a disaster may not be considered by the formula until a year or more after the disaster.[24]

WIOA Adult Activities

The WIOA-DW program operates in partnership with WIOA Adult Activities (WIOA-AA), a separate grant program. WIOA-AA provides

---

[24] WIOA-DW formula grants are awarded on a program-year basis (July 1-June 30). Grants are calculated using unemployment factors for the 12-month period ending 9 months prior to the program year. For example, grants for program year 2017 (beginning July 1, 2017) were based on the 12-month period ending September 30, 2016.

federal formula grants to states to support career services and training activities that are similar to those supported through the WIOA-DW program. Services under both WIOA-DW and WIOA-AA are typically provided by the same state agency at the same physical location.

Unlike WIOA-DW funding, which is limited to a statutory definition of dislocated workers, WIOA-AA funding can be used to serve any jobseeker over the age of 18, including new labor force entrants and incumbent workers. Because eligibility for WIOA-AA benefits does not require job loss, the program does not fit this chapter's criteria for inclusion. Still, WIOA-AA benefits may provide career services and training benefits to disaster-affected workers whose job loss or job interruption does not meet the WIOA-DW definition.

Disaster Dislocated Worker Grants[25]

Disaster Dislocated Worker Grants (DDWGs) are grants that support *disaster relief employment*: temporary disaster recovery jobs for disaster-affected workers. In some cases, DDWGs can also support career services and training for participants already enrolled in temporary jobs or persons who have relocated due to a disaster.

Financing and Administration

DDWGs are one of several types of National Dislocated Worker Grants (NDWGs).[26] NDWGs are supported by a 20% reservation from the WIOA dislocated worker appropriation. DOL has the discretion to determine the portion of NDWGs that will be used for DDWGs. NDWGs are authorized by Section 170 of WIOA.

---

[25] While these grants are authorized in Section 170 of WIOA, DOL guidance has offered more detail. Much of the information in this section is from DOL Training and Employment Guidance Letter 02-15, issued July 1, 2015. For the full document, see https://wdr.doleta.gov/directives/corr_doc.cfm?docn=4439.

[26] NDWGs can also support states that experience plant closures, mass layoffs, or higher-than-average demand for employment and training services for dislocated military services members or spouses.

DDWGs applications must be submitted by the state or territorial agency that receives WIOADW formula funds.[27] States may initially apply for DDWGs using an abbreviated Emergency Application, which should be submitted within 15 days of the qualifying declaration. The state applicant must submit a full application within 60 days. While state agencies are the grantee, they may subgrant funds to local workforce development boards or expend funds through public and private agencies engaged in qualified projects.

Qualifying Events

DDWG funds can be awarded to states that experience an emergency or major disaster as declared under the Stafford Act or by a federal agency. States may also qualify for a grant if a substantial number of individuals (at least 50) relocated to the state or area from a federally declared disaster area.

Individual Eligibility

Individuals eligible for disaster relief employment must either reside in the disaster-affected area or have been forced to relocate due to the disaster. In addition, cligible workers must be

- a dislocated worker as defined in Section 3(15) of WIOA,
- a long-term unemployed individual as defined by the state,
- temporarily or permanently laid off as a consequence of the disaster, or
- a self-employed individual who become unemployed or significantly underemployed as a result of the disaster.[28]

Supported Services and Benefits

DDWGs primarily support Disaster Relief Employment: temporary jobs that respond to the disaster. Generally, these positions can be clean-up and

---

[27] Because American Samoa, Guam, the Northern Mariana Islands, Palau, Puerto Rico, and the U.S. Virgin Islands receive WIOA-DW funds, these jurisdictions are eligible for apply for DDWG funds.

[28] See WIOA Section 170(d).

recovery efforts such as demolition, repair, or reconstruction. Eligible temporary jobs can also include humanitarian efforts such as the distribution of food, clothing, or other provisions.[29]

Workers employed in Disaster Relief Employment must be paid wages that are the higher of the federal, state, or local minimum wage, or the comparable rate of pay for similar workers at the same employer. In most cases, a participant may not hold a temporary job for longer than 12 months or 2,080 hours.

DDWGs can also support career and training services for dislocated workers who are already participating in temporary jobs and are unlikely to return to their prior employment. In cases where a DDWG is awarded on the basis of relocated workers, career and training services will be the primary services because eligible workers have relocated to outside the disaster area.

POLICY CONSIDERATIONS AND PRIOR TEMPORARY MODIFICATIONS

When considering disaster response programs, it can be useful to consider funding mechanisms (e.g., federal appropriations or state taxes), funding limitations (e.g., capped or entitlements), and whether a program is designed as an immediate benefit or a longer-term investment. In the past, Congress has enacted legislation in response to some of these issues and program limitations.

Funding Mechanisms and Limitations UC and DUA Funding

In budgetary terms, UC benefits are an entitlement (although the program is financed by a dedicated state tax imposed on employers in the state and not by general revenue). Similarly, DUA benefits are paid from

[29] DDWG funds can only support work related to humanitarian work, they cannot cover the humanitarian aid itself (e.g., food).

federal funds appropriated for the DRF and have always been paid to individuals who meet the eligibility requirements in a manner similar to an entitlement. While funding for the DRF depends upon the appropriations process, when the balance of the DRF becomes low, Congress has always provided additional funding through both annual and supplemental appropriations to replenish the account. Consequently, both UC and DUA have the ability to rapidly respond to unemployment caused by disasters and provide immediate income support to the unemployed.

However, increased UC outlays may potentially trigger increases on SUTA or FUTA taxes on the affected state's employers because even if a state's trust fund account is depleted, the state remains legally required to continue paying benefits. Such a state may need to raise SUTA taxes on its employers or reduce UC benefit levels. Alternatively, a state might borrow money either from the dedicated loan account within the UTF or from outside sources. If a state chooses to borrow funds from the UTF, not only will the state be required to continue paying benefits, it also will be required to repay the funds (plus any interest due) it has borrowed from the federal loan account. If the loans are not repaid within approximately two years, an increase in the net FUTA taxes faced by the state's employers may be triggered.[30]

In the past, Congress has enacted temporary measures to address high levels of UC claims and corresponding stress on state UC trust funds after a disaster. After Hurricane Katrina, Congress enacted the QI, TMA, and Abstinence Programs Extension and Hurricane Katrina Unemployment Relief Act of 2005 (P.L. 109-91), which transferred $500 million from the Federal Unemployment Account of the UTF to the state accounts of Alabama ($15 million), Louisiana ($400 million), and Mississippi ($85 million). This helped to alleviate the burden of the increased UC claims and prevent or dampen automatic SUTA tax increases that would have otherwise occurred in response to increased state UC outlays.

More recently, Congress enacted the Bipartisan Budget Act of 2018 (P.L. 115-123). Among other provisions, P.L. 115-123 included Section

---

[30] For full details on the mechanics of loans, see CRS Report RS22954, The Unemployment Trust Fund (UTF): State Insolvency and Federal Loans to States.

20801, which authorized a deferral of interest payments on an outstanding federal UI loan for the U.S. Virgin Islands.

WIOA-DW and DDWG Funding

WIOA-DW and DDWG activities are supported by annual discretionary appropriations and associated activities are constrained by appropriations levels. In some cases, Congress has appropriated additional funds for these activities in disaster-related areas, though funding is not automatic and, because it must be appropriated, it is likely to be less timely than UC or DUA. Whether or not Congress appropriates supplemental funds, states have some flexibility to direct WIOA-DW funds to disaster-affected areas (particularly through the governor's reserve) and DOL has some discretion in awarding DDWG funds. DOL can, for example, choose to direct a larger portion of the National Dislocated Worker Set-Aside to DDWG activities, but it is still subject to annual funding limits and prioritizing DDWG activities will likely mean less funding for other National Dislocated Worker activities.[31]

Funding for workforce services has been expanded temporarily through additional appropriations that supplemented regular annual appropriations. In 2005, the Department of Defense, Emergency Supplemental Appropriations to Address Hurricanes in the Gulf of Mexico, and Pandemic Influenza Act (P.L. 109-148) appropriated $125 million in supplemental funds for National Emergency Grants (a precursor to DDWGs) "related to the consequences of hurricanes in the Gulf of Mexico in calendar year 2005," of which Hurricane Katrina was the most severe.

More recently, the aforementioned P.L. 115-123 appropriated $100 million to the dislocated worker national reserve (the intermediate funding stream that supports DDWGs) for expenses directly related to the consequences of Hurricanes Harvey, Maria, and Irma and for those

[31] For example, in September 2017, DOL canceled a prior solicitation for "Dislocated Worker Opportunity Grants" noting that funds had been redirected to Hurricane Harvey response; see TEGL 17-01, Change 2, https://wdr.doleta.gov/directives/attach/TEGL/TEGL_117_Change_2.pdf.

jurisdictions that received a major disaster declaration due to wildfires in 2017.

Immediate Benefits vs. Longer-Term Investment

UC and DUA benefits usually offer the advantage of getting assistance to affected workers quickly, but benefits are of limited duration. Conversely, WIOA-DW and DDWG may offer less immediate relief, but may function as a longer-term investment in disaster-affected communities.

Income Support: Prompt Benefit, Limited Duration

Both UC and DUA benefits are structured to rapidly respond to economic conditions (caused by a disaster in the case of DUA) and provide immediate income support to the unemployed. In particular, each state agency responsible for administration of the UC program is assessed in part on the state's "methods of administration" to ensure that eligible claimants are paid UC benefits promptly when determined to be eligible.[32] While these benefits can typically be provided quickly, it should be noted that the prompt payment of both UC and DUA benefits is dependent on a functioning state UC program. If the administrative abilities of the state offices are impacted by the disaster—as occurred in Louisiana after Hurricane Katrina and has also been experienced after the series of 2017 hurricanes in Puerto Rico and the U.S. Virgin Islands—the processing of claims and subsequent payment of benefits may be delayed.[33]

---

[32] For detailed information on how states must ensure their methods of administration of the UC program conform to federal requirements see https://workforcesecurity.doleta.gov/unemploy/conformity-payment.asp.

[33] Jeffery Bartash, "Puerto Ricans put out of work by hurricane can't even apply for unemployment benefits," *Market Watch,* October 12, 2017, https://www. marketwatch.com/story/puerto-ricans-put-out-of-work-by-hurricane-cant-even apply-for-unemployment-benefits-2017-10-12. Ernice Gilbert, "Dept. of Labor Says Being Understaffed Means it's Unable to take Action Against Employers who Neglect Unemployment Insurance Payments," *The Virgin Islands Consortium*, January 30, 2018, http://viconsortium.com/business/dept-of-labor-says-being-understaffed-means-itsunable-to-take-action-against-employers-who-neglect-unemployment-insurance-payments/.

UC and DUA are available for a limited duration. UC is limited by state policy and is typically limited to 26 weeks.[34] DUA assistance is available to eligible individuals as long as the major disaster continues, but no longer than 26 weeks after the disaster declaration.

After Hurricane Katrina, Congress enacted the Katrina Emergency Assistance Act of 2006 (P.L. 109-176). Section 2 of this law extended DUA benefits for persons eligible under the Stafford Act due to Hurricane Katrina or Hurricane Rita for an additional 13 weeks, for a total of 39 weeks of potential benefits. Workers who exhausted their UC benefits but had received less than a total of 39 weeks of benefits would receive DUA benefits for as many weeks as necessary to reach a total of 39 weeks of UC and DUA benefits combined. This extension did not apply to any subsequent major disasters.

Workforce Programs: Less Timely, Longer-term Investment

The WIOA-DW program's general strategy of preparing dislocated workers for locally in-demand jobs may offer limited short-term value, especially if large numbers of local worksites are disrupted due to the disaster. WIOA-DW activities could, however, be viewed as a longer-term investment in preparing dislocated workers for an area's post-disaster labor market.

Disaster relief employment under DDWG is designed to respond to labor market disruptions by providing dislocated workers with federally subsidized employment while local labor markets recover. It may provide a more-immediate benefit than WIOA-DW activities, but the time necessary to award a DDWG, recruit workers, begin work, and pay the workers may create some time gap between a disaster and federal resources reaching workers.[35] The 12-month maximum duration of disaster relief employment, however, may offer a longer benefit window than UC and/or DUA.

---

[34] If a state meets certain unemployment measures, the permanent Extended Benefit program can provide an additional 13 weeks of federally funded benefits. For more information, see the "Extended Benefit Programs" section of CRS Report RL33362, *Unemployment Insurance: Programs and Benefits*.

[35] For example, Hurricane Irma made landfall in southern Florida around September 9, 2017. Broward County, FL, solicited workers for DDWG disaster relief employment on October 4,

Permanent law specifies that, in some cases, disaster relief employment under DDWGs can be extended past the original 12-month maximum for an additional 12 months. Supplemental appropriations can also extend the window for these programs. For example, the additional funds appropriated in the aforementioned P.L. 115-123 specified that the funds would be available through September 30, 2019, more than two years after the landfall of the 2017 hurricanes.

2017. See http://www.careersourcebroward.com/Portals/0/Home/NewsReleaseCSBDDisasterJobs_2017-10-02.pdf.

In: Unemployment Insurance
Editor: Arlette Bolk
ISBN: 978-1-53614-937-1

Chapter 5

RECENT LEGISLATIVE AND REGULATORY DEVELOPMENTS IN STATES' ABILITY TO DRUG TEST UNEMPLOYMENT COMPENSATION APPLICANTS AND BENEFICIARIES*

Julie M. Whittaker

Federal law permits states to restrict an individual's Unemployment Compensation (UC) benefit eligibility for certain circumstances related to the "fact or cause" of unemployment; this includes situations in which an individual was fired for drug use or refusing to take a drug test. Most states have specific disqualifications for drug-related job loss (see Table 5-8 in the hyperlink), including reporting to work under the influence of drugs/alcohol; violating the employer's drug policy, including refusing to undergo drug or alcohol testing; or having tested positive for drugs or alcohol under certain

* This is an edited, reformatted and augmented version of Congressional Research Service, Publication No. IN10909, dated May 23, 2018.

circumstances. Proposals to expand drug testing in the UC program have been considered in recent (113th, 114th, and 115th) Congresses. Interest in these proposals has been balanced by concerns that federal or state laws may be subject to a constitutional challenge if UC eligibility determination or ongoing receipt of UC benefits requires passing drug tests without taking into account individualized suspicion of illicit drug use.

Recent developments to expand the states' ability to drug test UC applicants and beneficiaries include the enactment of a law permitting two new types of drug testing, the issuance of guidance and regulations to support the implementation of the law, the overturning of these regulations, and the Trump Administration's announcement of intent to propose a new drug testing rule.

New Permissible Types of Drug Testing: P.L. 112-96

Section 2105 of the Middle Class Tax Relief and Job Creation Act of 2012 (P.L. 112-96; February 22, 2012) amended federal law to allow states to conduct two types of drug testing. First, it expanded the longstanding state option to disqualify UC applicants who were discharged from employment with their most recent employer (as defined under state law) for unlawful drug use by allowing states to drug test these applicants to determine UC benefit eligibility or disqualification. Second, it allowed states to drug test UC applicants for whom suitable work (as defined under state law) is available only in an occupation that regularly conducts drug testing, to be determined under new regulations issued by the Secretary of Labor.

Program Guidance

In response to P.L. 112-96, the U.S. Department of Labor (DOL) released guidance—Unemployment Insurance Program Letter (UIPL), No. 1-15, "Permissible Drug Testing of Certain Unemployment Compensation Applicants Provided for in Title II, Subtitle A of the Middle Class Tax Relief and Job Creation Act of 2012—on October 1, 2014. This guidance (which remains in effect at this time) provided states direction on how to conduct drug testing of UC applicants who are discharged from employment with their most recent employer because of illegal use of controlled substances. States are permitted to deny benefits to individuals under these circumstances. According to DOL, three states have enacted such laws: Mississippi, Texas, and Wisconsin (see pp. 5-19 and 5-20 in the hyperlink).

New Regulations

As called for in P.L. 112-96, on August 1, 2016, DOL promulgated 20 C.F.R. Part 620, a new rule to implement the provisions of the law relating to the drug testing of UC applicants for whom suitable work (as defined under state law) is available only in an occupation that regularly conducts drug testing. The rule provided a list of the applicable occupations (20 C.F.R. §620.3) that regularly conduct drug testing. Significantly, the section of the regulations following this list (20 C.F.R. §620.4) limited a state's ability to conduct a drug test on UC applicants to those individuals who are only available for work in an occupation that regularly conducts drug testing under 20 C.F.R. §620.3. Thus, although an individual's previous occupation may have been listed in 20 C.F.R. §620.3, as long as the individual was currently able, available, and searching for work in at least one occupation not listed in 20 C.F.R. §620.3, the individual could not be subject to drug testing to determine eligibility for UC (unless the individual had been discharged because of a drug-related discharge).

Repeal of Drug Testing Regulation Using Congressional Review Act: H.J.Res. 42/P.L. 115-17

Various stakeholders have voiced concerns about the UC drug testing provisions enacted under P.L. 112- 96 and about the DOL rule finalized under 20 C.F.R. Part 620. For example, advocates for UC beneficiaries claimed that drug testing applicants did not address any policy problem, while a state administration stakeholder group, as well as some Members of the House Ways and Means Committee, pushed for a broader interpretation and more flexibility in implementing drug testing than was offered under the DOL rule. On September 7, 2016, a hearing on Unemployment Insurance included statements by Representative Kevin Brady that expanded upon his disagreement with the DOL rule and its narrow interpretation.

Policy consideration then turned to using the Congressional Review Act (CRA) to overturn 20 C.F.R. Part 620. On January 1, 2017, Representative Kevin Brady introduced such a CRA resolution: H.J.Res. 42, which was passed by the House on February 15, 2017, and passed by the Senate on March 14, 2017. President Trump signed H.J.Res. 42/P.L. 115-17 on March 31, 2017. Since a list of occupations that requires drug testing no longer exists within the *Code of Federal Regulations* (on account of P.L. 115-17), the ability to prospectively test UC claimants based upon occupation is no longer available to states. Without this rule, states currently may drug test UC claimants only if they were discharged from employment because of either unlawful drug use or for refusing a drug test.

On February 15, 2017, in the *Congressional Record*, several members provided justification for their support or opposition of the measure. Representative Kevin Brady, among others, supported the measure. He argued the intent of P.L. 112-96 was to provide states the ability to determine how to best implement drug testing programs but the final regulation narrowed the law to circumstances where testing is legally required (rather than the broader definition of generally required by employer) and removed state discretion in conducting drug testing in their UC programs. Representative Richard E. Neal, among others, argued in opposition of the measure, stating there was no evidence that unemployed workers have higher rates of drug abuse than the general population and that it appeared that some states may be trying to limit the number of workers who collect UC benefits.

AGENDA NOTICE OF PROPOSED RULEMAKING

In spring 2018, the President's Unified Agenda of Regulatory and Deregulatory Actions (Agenda) proposed to issue a Notice of Proposed Rulemaking from DOL that is to identify the occupations that regularly conduct drug testing for purposes of Section 2105 of P.L. 112-96.

On April 17, 2018, at the House Committee on Ways and Means Hearing on Jobs and Opportunity: Federal Perspectives on the Jobs Gap, Chairman Brady asked Labor Secretary Acosta about the status of crafting new regulations on drug testing UC applicants (see the hyperlink beginning at 1 hour, 56 minutes). Secretary Acosta replied that DOL was in the process of drafting a new proposed rule, but that it had to take into consideration the reissue requirements of the Congressional Review Act. The CRA prohibits an agency from reissuing the rule in "substantially the same form" or issuing a "new rule that is substantially the same" as the disapproved rule, "unless the reissued or new rule is specifically authorized by a law enacted after the date of the joint resolution disapproving the original rule."

In: Unemployment Insurance
Editor: Arlette Bolk

ISBN: 978-1-53614-937-1

Chapter 6

THE UNEMPLOYMENT TRUST FUND (UTF): STATE INSOLVENCY AND FEDERAL LOANS TO STATES*

Julie M. Whittaker

SUMMARY

Although states have a great deal of autonomy in how they establish and run their unemployment insurance programs, federal law requires states to pay Unemployment Compensation (UC) benefits promptly as provided under state law. During some recessions, current taxes and reserve balances may be insufficient to cover state obligations for UC benefits. States may borrow funds from the federal loan account within the Unemployment Trust Fund (UTF) to meet UC benefit obligations.

This chapter summarizes how insolvent states may borrow funds from the UTF loan account to meet their UC benefit obligations. It includes the manner in which states must repay federal UTF loans. It also provides details on how the UTF loans may trigger potential interest accrual and

* This is an edited, reformatted and augmented version of Congressional Research Service, Publication No. IN10812, dated November 8, 2017.

explains the timetable for increased net Federal Unemployment Taxes Act (FUTA) taxes if the funds are not repaid promptly.

Outstanding loans listed by state may be found at the Department of Labor's (DOL's) website, https://ows.doleta.gov/unemploy/budget.asp.

UNEMPLOYMENT COMPENSATION, UNEMPLOYMENT TAXES, AND A STATE'S OBLIGATION TO PAY BENEFITS

Unemployment Compensation (UC) is a joint federal-state program financed by federal payroll taxes under the Federal Unemployment Tax Act[1] (FUTA) and by state payroll taxes under State Unemployment Tax Acts (SUTA).[2] These revenues are deposited into the appropriate account within the federal Unemployment Trust Fund (UTF).

Originally, the intent of the UC program, among other goals, was to help counter economic fluctuations such as recessions.[3] This intent is reflected in the current UC program's funding and benefit structure. When the economy grows, UC program revenue rises through increased tax revenues. At the same time, UC program spending falls because fewer workers are unemployed. The effect of collecting more taxes while decreasing spending on benefits dampens demand in the economy. It also creates a surplus of funds, or a *reserve fund*, for the UC program to draw upon during a recession. These reserve balances are credited in the state's account within the UTF. During an economic slowdown or recession, UC tax revenue falls and UC program spending rises as more workers lose their jobs and receive UC benefits. The increased amount of UC payments to unemployed workers

---

[1] §§ 3301-3311 of the Internal Revenue Code of 1986 (26 U.S.C. §§3301-33011). For a complete description of FUTA, see CRS Report R44527, *Unemployment Compensation: The Fundamentals of the Federal Unemployment Tax (FUTA)*.

[2] The underlying framework of the Unemployment Compensation (UC) program is contained in the Social Security Act (SSA). Title III of the SSA authorizes grants to states for the administration of state UC laws, Title IX authorizes the various components of the federal Unemployment Trust Fund (UTF), and Title XII authorizes advances or loans to insolvent state UC programs.

[3] See, for example, President Franklin Roosevelt's remarks at the signing of the SSA at http:// www.ssa.gov/history/fdrstmts.html#signing.

dampens the economic effect of lost earnings by injecting additional funds into the economy.

State and Federal Unemployment Taxes State Unemployment Taxes

States levy their own payroll taxes (SUTA) on employers to fund regular UC benefits and the state share (50%) of the Extended Benefit (EB) program.[4] Federal laws and regulations provide broad guidelines for these state taxes. Each state deposits its SUTA revenue into its account within the UTF.

SUTA revenue finances UC benefits. Generally, when economic activity is robust and increasing, SUTA revenue is greater than a state's UC expenditures. As a result, the state's reserves within the UTF grow. This trend is reversed during economic recessions and during the early economic recovery period, when the state's reserves are drawn down and new SUTA revenue does not always make up the shortfall.

If the recession is deep enough and if SUTA revenue is inadequate for long periods of time, states may have insufficient funds to pay for UC benefits. Federal law, which requires states to pay these benefits, provides a loan mechanism within the UTF framework that an insolvent state may opt to use to meet its UC benefit payment obligations.[5] States must pay back these loans. If the loans are not paid back quickly (depending on the timing of the beginning of the loan period), states may face interest charges and the states' employers may face increased net FUTA rates until the loans are repaid.

---

[4] The Extended Benefit (EB) program was established by the Federal-State Extended Unemployment Compensation Act of 1970 (EUCA), P.L. 91-373 (26 U.S.C. 3304, note). EUCA may extend receipt of unemployment benefits by 13 weeks or 20 weeks at the state level if certain economic situations exist within the state. For details, see CRS Report RL33362, *Unemployment Insurance: Programs and Benefits*.

[5] Federal unemployment compensation law does not restrict the states from using loan resources outside of the UTF. Depending on state law, states may have other funding measures available and may be able to use funds from outside of the UTF to pay the benefits (such as issuing bonds).

In the years immediately following the most recent recession, many states had insufficient SUTA revenue and UTF account balances to pay UC benefits.

Federal Unemployment Taxes

All FUTA revenue is deposited into the Employment Security Administration Account (ESAA) within the UTF. Federal unemployment taxes pay for the federal share of EB (50%) and for administrative grants to the states. Additionally, through the federal loan account within the UTF, FUTA funds may be loaned to insolvent states to assist the payment of the states' UC obligations.

Net FUTA Rate Is 0.6%

FUTA imposes a 6.0% gross federal unemployment tax rate on the first $7,000 paid annually by employers to each employee. Employers in states with programs approved by the U.S. Labor Secretary and with no outstanding federal loans may credit up to 5.4 percentage points of state unemployment taxes paid against the 6.0% tax rate, making the minimum net federal unemployment tax rate 0.6%.[6]

Because most employees earn more than the $7,000 taxable wage ceiling in a calendar year, the FUTA tax typically is $42 per worker per year ($7,000 × 0.6%), or just over 2 cents per hour for a full-time, year-round worker.[7]

---

[6] §3304 of FUTA (26 U.S.C. §3304) allows up to 5.4% credit for *actual* state unemployment taxes paid. Additionally, under §3303 of FUTA (26 U.S.C. §3303), employers that paid less than a 5.4% rate in state unemployment taxes are eligible for an *additional* state tax credit of up to 5.4%. The total state tax credit (actual and additional) on federal unemployment tax calculation is restricted to be no more than 5.4%. Thus, all employers in states with approved UC programs receive a 5.4% credit in the calculation of FUTA, even if the employer paid less than a 5.4% rate in state unemployment taxes.

[7] Assuming a full-time, year-round worker works 52 weeks per year and 40 hours per week (for 2,080 hours per year), 42 ÷ 2080 = $0.0202 and the state has no state tax credit reduction because of outstanding loans.

States Required to Pay UC Benefits

States have a great deal of autonomy in how they establish and run their unemployment insurance programs. However, the framework established by federal laws is clear and requires states to promptly pay the UC benefits as provided under state law.[8]

In budgetary terms, UC benefits are an entitlement (although the program is financed by a dedicated tax imposed on employers and not by general revenue). Thus, even if a recession hits a given state and, as a result, that state's trust fund account is depleted, the state remains legally required to continue paying benefits. To do so, the state might borrow money either from the dedicated loan account[9] within the UTF or from outside sources.

If the state chooses to borrow funds from the UTF, not only will the state be required to continue paying benefits, it also will be required to repay the funds (plus any interest due) it has borrowed from the federal loan account within a few years. Such states may need to raise taxes on their employers or reduce UC benefit levels, actions that dampen economic growth, job creation, and consumer demand. In short, states have strong incentives to keep adequate funds in their trust fund accounts.

If the state borrows from sources outside the UTF, the state would not be subject to the loan restrictions described below. Instead, the state would be subject to the terms within that outside loan agreement, which might offer a different (more favorable) interest rate or repayment schedule but may include fees to establish the loan.

---

[8] §3304 of FUTA (26 U.S.C. §3304). If the state does not pay the UC benefits, federal law is explicit. The state will not have a UC program meeting federal requirements, and thus the federal unemployment tax paid by employers on each employee's annual earnings would be a net tax of 6.0% (that is, up to $420 per worker with no allowable state tax credit) rather than 0.6% if the state UC program paid benefits and had no outstanding loans.

[9] The Federal Unemployment Account (FUA).

Funds Available for Loans to States Within the UTF

The Federal Unemployment Account (FUA) is the federal loan account within the UTF. Two automatic funding sources are available within the FUA. Additionally, the FUA may borrow funds from other federal accounts within the UTF or (if needed) from the general fund of the U.S. Treasury. From FY2009 to FY2015, the FUA had to borrow funds from the U.S. Treasury to finance loans to the state accounts.[10]

1. Excess revenue from the Extended Unemployment Compensation Account (EUCA) is deposited into the FUA.[11] In FY2018, the EUCA net balance is an estimated shortfall of (negative) $10.74 billion. Thus, no EUCA funds are projected to be distributed to the FUA in FY2018.
2. Revenue from additional FUTA taxes paid by employers when a reduced credit against federal unemployment taxes exists because the state has an outstanding unpaid loan from FUA is deposited into the FUA. (See the discussion below on "Federal Tax Increases on Outstanding Loans Through Credit Reductions" for a more detailed explanation of these additional taxes.)
3. Federal law allows the FUA to borrow available funds from the other federal (EUCA and ESAA) accounts within the UTF.[12]
4. Federal law also authorizes appropriations as loans from the general fund of the U.S. Treasury if balances in the federal accounts are

[10] The FUA completed repaying its general fund advance balance in June of 2015, and FUA funds have since been used to assist in repaying the remaining general fund advances to the EUCA. The EUCA is projected to finish repaying its general fund advance loans in FY2018 but will continue to owe funds to the FUA while slowly repaying those non-interest bearing loans from the FUA. The net FUA balance is projected to remain around $12.5 billion for the duration of the projection period, whereas the net EUCA balance is projected to remain negative through 2021 as repayments continue to be made to the FUA.

[11] Following federal law, at the end of every month 20% of all newly collected FUTA revenue is deposited into the EUCA, which is authorized to pay for the federal share of EB. The EUCA balance is limited to the maximum of 0.5% of covered wages ($31.44 billion in FY2018). If the EUCA balance exceeds the limitation, the excess is distributed to the FUA.

[12] 42 U.S.C. 1110.

insufficient to cover their expenditures.[13] (For example, if the states' borrowing needs exceed the available FUA balance.) Such appropriations require discretionary action by Congress and the President.

Mechanism for Receiving a Loan from the UTF

Once a state recognizes that it does not have sufficient funds to pay UC benefits, the mechanism for receiving a loan from the UTF is straightforward. The state's governor (or the governor's designee) must submit a letter requesting that the U.S. Labor Secretary advance funds to the state account within the UTF. Once the loan is approved by the U.S. Labor Secretary, the funds are placed into the state account in monthly increments.

Loan Repayment

States with outstanding loans from the UTF must repay them fully by the November 10 following the second consecutive January 1 on which the state has an outstanding loan. If the outstanding loan is not repaid by that time, the state will face an effective federal tax increase. Thus, a state may have approximately 22 months (if borrowing began on January 1) to 34 months (if borrowing began on January 2) to repay the loan without a federal tax increase, depending on when it obtained the outstanding loan.

As of February 15, 2018, approximately $1.3 billion in federal UTF loans to the states were outstanding. A current list of states with outstanding loans may be found at the Department of Labor's (DOL's) website, https://ows.doleta.gov/unemploy/budget.asp.

---

[13] 42 U.S.C. 1323.

Federal Tax Increases on Outstanding Loans Through Credit Reductions

If the state does not repay a loan by November 10 of the second year,[14] the state becomes subject to a reduction in the amount of state unemployment tax credit applied against the federal unemployment tax beginning with the preceding January 1 until the state repays the loan fully. Depending on the duration of the loan and certain other measures, one or more of three different credit reductions may be required. These reductions are fully catalogued in *Table 1*. At the height of the period following the most recent recession (2011), 20 states and the Virgin Islands faced increased FUTA rates because of outstanding UTF loans.[15]

Basic Credit Reduction

The credit reduction is initially a 0.3 percentage point reduction for the year beginning with the calendar year in which the second consecutive January 1 passes during which the loan is outstanding and increases by a 0.3 percentage point reduction for each year there is an outstanding loan. For example, in the first year, the credit reduction results in the net federal tax rate increasing from 0.6% to 0.9%—an additional $21 for each employee; in the second year, it would increase to 1.2%—a cumulative additional $42 for each employee.

Additional Credit Reductions: 2.7 Add-on and Benefit-Cost Ratio

Add-on

Two potential other credit reductions exist (in addition to the cumulative 0.3 percentage point increases) during the ensuing calendar years in which a state has an outstanding loan:

[14] The "second year" is the year when the state has outstanding UTF loans on January 1 for the second January 1 in a row. Depending on the timing when the first loan began, it may actually be the third year of the loan.

[15] See http://workforcesecurity.doleta.gov/unemploy/docs/reduced_credit_states.xlsx.

1. Beginning in the third year, the 2.7 add-on uses a statutory formula that takes into consideration the average annual wages and average employment contribution rate.[16]
2. Beginning in the fifth year, the Benefit-Cost Ratio (BCR) add-on replaces the 2.7 add-on and uses the five-year benefit-cost rate as well as average wages in its calculation. [17]

Table 1 presents these reductions and the subsequent net FUTA tax faced by state employers as a result of these unpaid loans. If any January 1 passes without an outstanding balance, the year count starts over with the next loan. DOL maintains a list of potential reduced credit states at http://workforcesecurity.doleta.gov/unemploy/docs/reduced_credit_states.xlsx.

Avoiding Some or All of the Credit Reduction

Section 272 of P.L. 97-248 allows a delinquent state the option of repaying—on or before November 9—a portion of its outstanding loans each year through transfer of a specified amount from its account in the UTF to the FUA.

If the state complies with all the requirements listed below, the potential credit reduction is avoided (there is no reduction):

- The state must repay all loans for the most recent one-year period ending on November 9, plus the potential additional taxes that would have been imposed for the tax year based upon a state tax credit reduction.
- The state must have sufficient amounts in the state account of the UTF to pay all compensation for the last quarter of that calendar year without receiving a loan.

---

[16] The 2.7 add-on formula is [(2.7% × 7000 ÷ U.S. Annual Average Wage) - Average Annual State Tax Rate on Total Wages] × State Annual Average Wage ÷ 7000.

[17] The Benefit-Cost Ratio (BCR) add-on formula is: Max [Five-year Average State Unemployment UC Outlays ÷ Taxable Wages, 2.7] - Average Annual State Unemployment Tax Rate on Total Wages.

- The state also must have altered its state law to increase the net solvency of its account with the UTF.

Table 1. Schedule of State Tax Credit Reduction and Net Federal Unemployment Tax Act (FUTA) Tax

Loan Year	Credit Reduction	Additional Reductions	Net FUTA Tax (0.6% + credit reductions)
Year 1 of outstanding loan	0.0%	None	0.6%
Year 2 (applied retroactively at end of calendar year)	0.3%	None	0.9%
Year 3	0.6%	2.7 Add-on	1.2% or more[a]
Year 4	0.9%	2.7 Add-on	1.5% or more[a]
Year 5	1.2%	BCR Add-on	1.8% or more[b]
Year 6	1.5%	BCR Add-on	2.1% or more[b]
Year 7	1.8%	BCR Add-on	2.4% or more[b]
Year 8	2.1%	BCR Add-on	2.7% or more[b]
Year 9	2.4%	BCR Add-on	3.0% or more[b]
Year 10	2.7%	BCR Add-on	3.3% or more[b]
Year 11	3.0%	BCR Add-on	3.6% or more[b]
Year 12	3.3%	BCR Add-on	3.9% or more[b]
Year 13	3.6%	BCR Add-on	4.2% or more[b]
Year 14	3.9%	BCR Add-on	4.5% or more[b]
Year 15	4.2%	BCR Add-on	4.8% or more[b]
Year 16	4.5%	BCR Add-on	5.1% or more[b]
Year 17	4.8%	BCR Add-on	5.4% or more[b]
Year 18	5.1%	BCR Add-on	5.7% or more[b]
Year 19	5.4%	BCR Add-on	6.0%

Source: U.S. Department of Labor, Employment and Training Administration.

Notes: 2.7 Add-on = [(2.7% X 7000 ÷ U.S. Annual Average Wage) - Average Annual State Tax Rate on Total Wages] X State Annual Average Wage ÷ 7000.

Benefit Cost Ratio (BCR) Add-on = Max [Five-year Average State Unemployment Compensation Outlays ÷ Taxable Wages, 2.7] - Average Annual State Unemployment Tax Rate on Total Wages.

[a] Exact tax depends upon 2.7 Add-on calculation and whether state qualified for avoidance.

[b] Exact net tax depends upon BCR Add-on calculation (or the 2.7 Add-on calculation, if the BCR Add-on is waived).

From 2011 through 2014, South Carolina met these requirements. As a result, employers in South Carolina were not subject to a state tax credit reduction in the calculation of their FUTA taxes. (Generally, employers in South Carolina would have paid more in state unemployment taxes to meet these requirements.)

Avoiding Credit Reduction: Cap

Once a state begins to have a credit reduction, the state may apply to have the reductions capped if the state meets four criteria:

- No legislative or other action in 12 months ending September 30 has been taken to decrease the state's unemployment tax effort. (A state cannot actively decrease its expected state unemployment tax revenue from current law.)
- No legislative or other action has been taken to decrease the net solvency of the state's trust fund account. (For example, the state would not be allowed to actively increase the average UC benefit amount from current law requirements.)
- Average state unemployment tax rate on total wages must exceed the five-year average benefit-cost rate on total wages.
- Balance of outstanding loans as of September 30 must not be greater than the balance three years before.

Waiving the BCR Add-on

The BCR add-on may be waived if the Secretary of Labor determines the state did not take legislative or other actions to decrease the net solvency of the state's trust fund account. The 2.7 add-on would then replace the BCR add-on.[18]

[18] California and the U.S. Virgin Islands applied for and received the BCR waiver for 2017. See http://workforcesecurity.doleta.gov/unemploy/docs/reduced_credit_states.xlsx.

Revenue from Credit Reductions Reduces State UTF Loans

The additional federal taxes attributable to the credit reduction are applied against the state's outstanding UTF loan. Thus, although technically employers are paying additional FUTA taxes, the additional tax pays off a state's debt. The state's employers will pay the additional federal taxes resulting from the credit reduction no later than January 31 of the next calendar year.

INTEREST CHARGES ON LOANS

Since April 1, 1982 (P.L. 97-35 as amended), states have been charged interest on new loans that are not repaid by the end of the fiscal year in which they were obtained.[19] (Before April 1, 1982, states could receive these loans interest free.)[20]

The interest is the same rate as that paid by the federal government on state reserves in the UTF for the quarter ending December 31 of the preceding year but not higher than 10% per annum. The interest rate for calendar year loans is determined by Section 1202(b)(4) of the Social

[19] Interest payments can be delayed up to 9 months (and no interest on the unpaid interest would accrue) if the most recent 12-month average unemployment rate (from September of the previous year to August of that year) is 13.5% or higher [42 U.S.C. §1322(b)(9)]. If the state's January through June average insured unemployment rate (IUR) in the previous year is 6.5% or higher, the state would be required to pay 25% of that current year's interest that is due calculations [42 U.S.C. §1322(b)(3)(C)]. (The IUR is the ratio of UC claimants divided by individuals in UC-covered jobs. It excludes unemployed workers who have exhausted their UC benefits and the self-employed.) The state then would pay the remaining 25% in each of the next three years. The remainder of the interest payment would be not be subject to additional interest.

[20] §2004 of P.L. 111-5 temporarily waived interest payments and the accrual of interest on loans. The interest payments that were due from the time of enactment (February 17, 2009) until December 31, 2010, were deemed to have been made. No interest on advances accrued during the period. Although interest did not accrue during this period, this did *not* absolve states from repaying the underlying loans. If a state did not pay back funds within the prescribed amount of time or make good progress as determined by the Labor Secretary, the state tax credit was reduced. On January 1, 2011, the calculation of interest reverted to permanent law on interest charges.

Security Act. The interest rate for a calendar year is the earnings yield on the UTF for the quarter ending December 31 of the previous calendar year. The U.S. Treasury Department calculated the fourth-quarter earnings yield in 2017 to be 2.2153%. Thus, loans made in calendar year 2018 are subject to an interest rate of 2.2153%.[21]

States may not pay the interest directly or indirectly from SUTA revenue or funds in their state account within the UTF. If a state does not repay the interest, or if it pays the interest with funds from SUTA taxes, DOL is required by federal law to refuse to certify that state's program as being in compliance with federal law.[22] Not being in compliance with federal unemployment law would mean that the state would not be eligible to receive administrative grants and its state employers would not receive the state unemployment tax credit in the calculation of their federal unemployment taxes.

States may borrow funds without interest from the UTF during the year. To receive these interest-free loans, the states must meet five conditions:

1. The states must repay the loans by September 30.
2. For those repaid (by September 30) loans to maintain their interest-free status, there cannot be any loans made to that state in October, November, or December of the calendar year of such an interest-free loan. If loans are made in the last quarter of the calendar year, the "interest-free" loans made in the previous fiscal year will retroactively accrue interest charges.
3. The states must meet funding goals relating to their account in the UTF, established under regulations issued by DOL.

---

[21] U.S. Department of Labor (DOL), Employment and Training Administration, *Interest Rate on Title XII Advances During Calendar Year (CY) 2018*, Training and Employment Notice (TEN) 13-17, February 5, 2018, https://wdr.doleta.gov/directives/attach/TEN/TEN_13-17_Acc.pdf.

[22] 26 U.S.C. §3304(a)(17) and 42 C.F.R. §503(c)(3).

Table 2. Outstanding Loan Balances, Interest Owed, and 2017 State Tax Credit Reduction (February 14, 2018)

State[a]	Outstanding Advance Balance ($)	Interest for FY2018 ($)	2017 Tax Credit Reduction (%)	2017 Net FUTA Tax (0.6% + credit reductions)
California[a]	$1,213,035,332	$8,181,545	2.1[b]	2.7
Virgin Islands[c]	75,844,427	557,312	2.1[b]	2.7
Totals	1,288,879,760	8,738,857		

Source: Congressional Research Service table prepared using data from the U.S. Bureau of Public Debt, http://www.treasurydirect.gov/govt/reports/tfmp/tfmp_advactivitiessched.htm, and the U.S. Department of Labor, http://ows.doleta.gov/unemploy/content/reduced_credit_states.xls.

Notes: States not listed on this table had no outstanding loans on February 14, 2018, had no outstanding interest accruals, and were not subject to a state tax credit reduction on the calculation of the net FUTA tax in 2017.

[a] Under UC law, the District of Columbia, Puerto Rico, and the Virgin Islands are considered to be states.

[b] For this year, the state received credit reduction add-on relief.

[c] P.L. 115-123 temporarily forgave the Virgin Islands for interest payments due in 2017 until September 28, 2018, and exempts that interest from accruing additional interest during this period.

In addition to these first three requirements, the phase-in of two new requirements began in 2014.[23] The full effect of the requirements will begin in 2019.[24]

---

[23] DOL, Employment and Training Administration, "Federal-State Unemployment Compensation Program Funding Goals for Interest-Free Loans," 75 *Federal Register* 57146, September 17, 2010.

[24] The DOL publishes an annual report on the details of each state's solvency measures used in the determination of interest-free loans. See DOL, Office of Unemployment Insurance, Employment and Training Administration, *State Unemployment Insurance Trust Fund Solvency Report*, 2017, https://ows.doleta.gov/unemploy/solvency.asp.

4. States must have had at least one year in the past five calendar years before the year in which advances are taken in which the Average High Cost Multiple[25] (AHCM) was greater than or equal to 1.0.
5. Additionally, states must meet two criteria for maintenance-of-tax effort in every year from the most recent year the AHCM was at least 1.0 and the year in which loans are taken.
   a The average state unemployment tax rate (total state unemployment tax amount collected over total taxable wages) was at least 80% of the prior year's rate.
   b The average state unemployment tax rate was at least 75% of the average benefit-cost ratio over the preceding five calendar years, where the benefit-cost ratio for a year is defined as the amount of benefits and interest paid in the year divided by the total covered wages paid in the year.

STATUS OF OUTSTANDING LOANS, ACCRUED INTEREST OWED, AND STATE TAX CREDIT REDUCTIONS

Table 2 lists all states that have outstanding loans.[26] The table also includes information on accrued interest payments for FY2017. The third column provides information on whether a state was subject to a credit reduction for tax year 2017. The last column provides the net FUTA tax faced by employers in each state that had an outstanding loan.

---

[25] The average high-cost multiple (AHCM) is the ratio of actual UTF account balances to the average of the 3 highest years of benefit payments experienced by the state over the past 20 years. Presumably, the average of the 3 highest years' outlays would be a good indicator of potential expected UC payments if another recession were to occur. Under these assumptions, if a state had saved enough funds to pay for an average high year of UC benefit activity, its AHCM would be at least 1.0.

[26] If a state is not listed on this table, (1) the state did not have any outstanding loans on February 14, 2018, (2) did not have interest accruals in FY2017, and (3) was not subject to a state tax credit reduction on the calculation of the net FUTA tax in 2017.

In: Unemployment Insurance
Editor: Arlette Bolk
ISBN: 978-1-53614-937-1

Chapter 7

PROGRAMS AVAILABLE TO UNEMPLOYED WORKERS THROUGH THE AMERICAN JOB CENTER NETWORK*

Benjamin Collins, David H. Bradley and Katelin P. Isaacs

ABSTRACT

Many federally funded programs that assist unemployed workers are co-located and coordinated through state-run American Job Centers (AJCs; also known as One-Stop Career Centers). The specific set of benefits and services available to a worker through the AJC network varies by the worker's characteristics and reason for unemployment.

Unemployment insurance (UI) is a federal-state system and mandatory AJC partner. UI benefits are available to workers who have involuntarily lost their jobs and have demonstrated a required level of labor force attachment. UI provides weekly cash payments to replace a portion of

* This is an edited, reformatted and augmented version of Congressional Research Service, Publication No. R43301, dated April 23, 2015.

eligible workers' earnings, up to a statewide maximum. Eligibility and benefit levels vary by state, though most states offer up to 26 weeks of state-financed UI benefits through each state's Unemployment Compensation (UC) program. Certain economic conditions may extend the duration of UI benefits through the permanent Extended Benefit (EB) program.

AJCs coordinate a number of reemployment programs that provide job search assistance and training subsidies. These programs include both broadly available programs and targeted programs. Unlike UI benefits, which are mandatory entitlements, these employment and training programs are subject to funding caps. The primary AJC partner programs can be characterized as follows:

- *Programs available to all jobseekers* do not have eligibility requirements, though they may have limited capacity. These programs provide varied job search, training, and educational services. They include adult activities supported under the Workforce Innovation and Opportunity Act of 2014 (WIOA; P.L. 113-128), which provide reemployment services and training vouchers; Employment Services (ES) under the Wagner-Peyser Act, which provide job search assistance and other non-training services to jobseekers; and adult education programs, which provide educational services at the secondary level and below.
- *Targeted programs* provide specialized services to certain populations. These services may be targeted by the circumstances of a worker's job loss or a worker's personal characteristics. Services provided through these programs can be more intensive or more readily available than those through programs with no eligibility requirements.

In addition to these primary programs, there are also several additional employment and training programs that are required AJC partners but are limited in scope and availability. The specific services offered by these additional programs vary, but tend to be targeted toward certain populations of jobseekers.

This chapter is limited to mandatory AJC partner programs under the Workforce Innovation and Opportunity Act of 2014. Some federally funded programs with employment and training components are not AJC partners. As such, the group of programs discussed in this chapter may vary from other reviews of federal workforce programs and should not be considered exhaustive.

Background on the American Job Center Network

Many federally funded programs to assist unemployed workers are coordinated through state-run American Job Centers (AJCs; also known as One-Stop Career Centers).[1] There are approximately 2,500 AJCs nationwide. Programs available to jobseekers at AJCs include income support (typically unemployment insurance), as well as a variety of reemployment and training services. Services may be provided on-site at an AJC or by a partner entity at a different location.

The specific set of services and benefits available to a worker through the AJC system varies by the worker's characteristics and reason for unemployment. Some programs are only available to target populations (e.g., veterans or workers with disabilities), while others are available to all jobseekers. The availability of employment and training services can also be limited by an AJC's capacity and financial resources.

The AJC/One-Stop system was established by the Workforce Investment Act of 1998 (WIA; P.L. 105-220). The Workforce Innovation and Opportunity Act of 2014 (WIOA; P.L. 113-128) amended and reauthorized many WIA programs and maintained the One-Stop/AJC system.

This chapter will provide a brief overview of the AJC mandatory partner programs. It begins with a discussion of unemployment insurance, a federal-state cooperative program that provides income support to unemployed workers. The subsequent sections discuss employment and training programs. These programs provide career counseling, job search assistance, occupational skills training, and other services to improve jobseekers' performance in the labor market.

---

[1] In June 2012, the Department of Labor announced an initiative to unify One-Stop Career Centers under the brand of the American Job Center network. More information on the implementation of the AJC network brand is available in Department of Labor Training and Employment Guidance Letter No. 36-11 at http://wdr.doleta.gov/directives/attach/TEGL/TEGL_36_11.Acc.pdf.

This chapter aims to offer a brief overview of the programs administered through the AJC system. It emphasizes eligibility requirements and the scope of benefits and services available to individuals. It does not emphasize the roles and responsibilities of institutional actors such as state agency grantees and local workforce boards.

NOTE ON THE PROGRAMS DISCUSSED

This chapter discusses mandatory partner programs in the AJC/One-Stop system as specified by Section 121 of the WIOA. Some federally funded programs with employment and training components are not required partners with AJCs and therefore are not discussed in this section. As such, the group of programs included in this chapter may vary from other reviews of federal employment training programs and should not be considered exhaustive.

UNEMPLOYMENT INSURANCE[2]

Unemployment insurance (UI) provides a weekly cash payment to workers who involuntarily become unemployed after establishing a requisite work history. There are two programs currently authorized within the UI system:

- Unemployment Compensation (UC)
- Extended Benefits (EB)

Federal laws and regulations provide broad guidelines on UC benefit coverage, eligibility, and benefit determination. The specifics of regular UC

[2] For additional background, see CRS Report RL33362, *Unemployment Insurance: Programs and Benefits*, by Julie M. Whittaker and Katelin P. Isaacs.

benefits are determined by each state. This results in essentially 53 different programs.[3]

Table 1. Unemployment Insurance Expenditures by Program Component, FY2014

Program Component	Description	FY2014 Outlays
State-financed UI expenditures		
Unemployment Compensation (UC)	Provides weekly cash payment to eligible, unemployed workers.	$35.9 billion
Federally financed UI expenditures		
Emergency Unemployment Compensation (EUC08) (now expired)	Until its expiration the week ending on or before January 1, 2014 (i.e., December 28, 2013; or December 29, 2013, in New York State), provided weekly cash payment to eligible, unemployed workers who had exhausted UC benefits. Availability and duration varied by state economic conditions.	$4.8 billion
Extended Benefits (EB)	Provides weekly cash payment to eligible, unemployed workers who have exhausted UC and EUC08 benefits. Availability and duration varies by state economic conditions.	$0.0 billion
UI Administrative Costs	Funds to states to administer UI benefits and programs.	$4.4 billion

Source: U.S. Department of Labor, *UI Outlook, President's* ***Budget*** FY2016, February 2015 at http://www.workforcesecurity.doleta.gov/unemploy/pdf/prez_budget.pdf.

Notes: UC, EUC08, and EB benefits are mandatory entitlements. Annual expenditures on these benefits vary by number of claimants and duration of benefits. The EUC08 program expired the week ending on or before January 1, 2014; no EUC08 benefits were payable after that date (i.e., December 28, 2013; or December 29, 2013, in New York State). No state met the conditions for EB benefits to be payable in FY2014. Under permanent law (P.L. 91-373), EB benefits are financed 50% by states and 50% by the federal government. P.L. 111-5, as amended, temporarily altered this federal-state funding arrangement through December 31, 2013, with the exception of "non-sharable" benefits (generally, these are former state and local employees' EB benefits). This temporary EB financing arrangement has now expired. Federal grants for UI administrative costs are appropriated.

[3] In limited circumstances, individuals who become unemployed due to a declared disaster and are not eligible for UC benefits in their state may be eligible for income support through the federal Disaster Unemployment Insurance (DUA) program. DUA is not a mandatory AJC partner. More information on DUA is available in CRS Report RS22022, *Disaster Unemployment Assistance (DUA)*, by Julie M. Whittaker.

When eligible workers lose their jobs, the UC program may provide income support through the payment of UC benefits. Individuals who exhaust UC benefits may be eligible for additional weeks of UI benefits through the permanent EB program.

Until its expiration at the end of December 2013, the temporary Emergency Unemployment Compensation (EUC08) program also provided additional weeks of UI benefits.[4] No benefits from the EUC08 program are currently available.

Table 1 provides data on recent outlays from the UC, EUC08, and EB programs.

Unemployment Compensation

The cornerstone of an unemployed worker's income security is the joint federal-state UC program,[5] which provides income support through the payment of UC benefits. The UC program pays benefits to covered workers who become involuntarily unemployed for economic reasons and meet state-established eligibility rules. The UC program generally does not provide UC benefits to the self-employed, those who are unable to work, or those who do not have a recent earnings history. States usually disqualify claimants who lost their jobs because of inability to work, unavailability for work, or a labor dispute. Workers are also typically ineligible if they voluntarily quit without good cause, were discharged for job-related misconduct, or refused suitable work without good cause. To receive UC benefits, claimants must have enough recent earnings to meet their state's earnings requirements.

---

[4] For additional details on the availability of EUC08 benefits prior to expiration, see CRS Report R42444, *Emergency Unemployment Compensation (EUC08): Status of Benefits Prior to Expiration*, by Katelin P. Isaacs and Julie M. Whittaker.

[5] For more information on UC, see CRS Report RS22538, *Unemployment Compensation: The Cornerstone of Income Support for Unemployed Workers*, by Julie M. Whittaker, and CRS Report RL33362, *Unemployment Insurance: Programs and Benefits*, by Julie M. Whittaker and Katelin P. Isaacs.

UC is financed by federal taxes under the Federal Unemployment Tax Act (FUTA) and by state payroll taxes under the State Unemployment Tax Acts (SUTA). Maximum weekly benefit amounts in January 2015 ranged from $133 (Puerto Rico) to $698 (Massachusetts) and, in states that provide dependent's allowances, up to $1,047 (Massachusetts). In February 2015, the average weekly benefit was $316. In most states, regular UC benefits are available for up to 26 weeks.[6]

Extended Benefits

The EB program, established by P.L. 91-373 (26 U.S.C. 3304 note), may extend UC benefits at the state level if certain economic conditions exist within the state. The EB program is permanently authorized, and is triggered when a state's insured unemployment rate (IUR) or total unemployment rate (TUR) reaches certain levels. All states must pay up to 13 weeks of EB if the IUR for the previous 13 weeks is at least 5% and is 120% of the average of the rates for the same 13-week period in each of the two previous years. There are two other optional thresholds that states may choose. If the state has chosen a given option, they would provide the following:

- Option 1: an additional 13 weeks of benefits if the state's IUR is at least 6%, regardless of previous years' averages.
- Option 2: an additional 13 weeks of benefits if the state's TUR is at least 6.5% and is at least 110% of the state's average TUR for the same 13-week period in either of the previous two years; an additional 20 weeks of benefits if the TUR is at least 8%.[7]

---

[6] For information on states that have enacted reductions in UC maximum duration, see CRS Report R41859, *Unemployment Insurance: Consequences of Changes in State Unemployment Compensation Laws*, by Katelin P. Isaacs.

[7] P.L. 111-312 made some temporary, technical changes to certain triggers in the EB program. P.L. 111-312, as amended, allows states to temporarily use lookback calculations based on three years of unemployment rate data (rather than the current lookback of two years of data) as part of their mandatory IUR and optional TUR triggers if states would otherwise trigger off or not be on a period of EB benefits. Using a two-year vs. a three-year EB trigger lookback

In addition to all state requirements for regular UC eligibility, the EB program requires claimants to have at least 20 weeks of full-time insured employment or the equivalent in their base period, and to conduct a systematic and sustained work search.[8] A current listing of states that have triggered on for EB can be found at http://www.workforcesecurity.doleta.gov/unemploy/ claims_arch.asp.

Under the 2009 stimulus package (P.L. 111-5), as amended, the federal government temporarily financed 100% of the EB program through December 31, 2013. This temporary EB financing provision has now expired. Under permanent law, the federal government finances 50% of the EB program and states finance the other 50%.

EMPLOYMENT AND TRAINING PROGRAMS

The AJC network co-locates and coordinates federally-funded employment and training programs. Services under these programs range from self-service (e.g., provision of computerized job listings) to more intensive case management and job training. Unlike UI, funding levels for employment and training programs are capped by statute or appropriation level. As such, it is possible that a jobseeker who is eligible for a program may not receive services.

This section divides the primary AJC partner programs into three groups:

---

is an important adjustment because some states are likely to trigger off of their EB periods in the near future despite high, sustained—but not increasing—unemployment rates.

States implement the lookback changes individually by amending their state UC laws. These state law changes must be written in such a way that if the two-year lookback is working and the state would have an active EB program, no action would be taken. But if a two-year lookback is not working as part of an EB trigger and the state is not triggered on to an EB period, then the state would be able to use a three-year lookback. This temporary option to use three-year EB trigger lookbacks expires the week on or before December 31, 2013.

[8] The base period is the time period during which wages earned and/or hours/weeks worked are examined to determine a worker's monetary entitlement to UI. Almost all states use the first 4 of the last 5 completed calendar quarters preceding the filing of the claim as their base period.

- *Programs available to all jobseekers*, which have no eligibility criteria;
- *Programs targeted by circumstances of job loss*, which provide services to workers whose job loss and work history meet certain conditions; and
- *Programs targeted by jobseeker characteristics*, which provide services to workers based on their personal characteristics rather than their work history or reason for unemployment.

Table 2. Eligibility Criteria for Employment and Training Programs Available through the American Job Center Network

Programs Available to All Jobseekers
• *All jobseekers* are eligible for job search assistance and training benefits under the Adult Activities provisions of the Workforce Innovation and Opportunity Act (WIOA) and basic education and English literacy courses through the Adult Education and Family Literacy Act (AEFLA).
• *All recipients of unemployment insurance* (UI) receive job matching and other employment services, funded under the Wagner-Peyser Act. Non-UI recipients may also receive these services.
Programs Targeted by Circumstance of Job Loss
• *Workers who were (1) involuntarily terminated, (2) well-attached to the labor force, and (3) unlikely to return to their previous occupation or industry* are eligible for job search assistance and training benefits under the Dislocated Worker provisions of WIOA.
• *Workers whose job loss is attributable to foreign trade* may be eligible for training and other benefits through the Trade Adjustment Assistance program.

Programs Targeted by Jobseeker Characteristics

- *Individuals with disabilities* may be eligible for customized services (including training) through state vocational rehabilitation programs.

Programs Targeted by Jobseeker Characteristics

- *Disadvantaged youth* may be eligible for services under the Youth Activities provisions of WIOA or placement in the residential Job Corps program.
- *Individuals age 55 or over* may be eligible for subsidized part-time employment through the Community Service Employment for Older Americans program.
- *Veterans* are eligible for job search assistance and other services through programs funded by the Jobs for Veterans State Grants.

Source: CRS review of eligibility criteria for listed programs.

Notes: Due to funding constraints, not all eligible individuals may actually receive benefits and services under each program. Additional services through competitive grants and other programs may also be available through the AJC network.

Table 2 summarizes the eligibility criteria for these primary partner programs, each of which is a formula grant program. In addition to these three groups of formula grant programs, there are also several additional programs that are required AJC partners but that are not available at all AJC locations. These additional programs are discussed in the final section of this chapter.

The remainder of this chapter discusses AJC mandatory partner programs, grouped by their eligibility criteria. Within each section, programs are discussed in descending order of their FY2015 funding level. Table 3 at the end of this chapter provides brief descriptions of each AJC partner program as well as their FY2015 funding levels.

Programs Available to All Jobseekers

The employment and training programs discussed in this section are funded by formula grants to states and do not have eligibility requirements. Funding levels are capped by annual appropriation levels. Job seekers may receive less intensive services or be placed on a waiting list due to limited resources.

Adult Employment and Training Activities

This WIOA-authorized formula grant program provides funds to states for employment and training services for both unemployed and underemployed individuals ages 18 and older. It is a universal access system with no additional eligibility requirements other than age.[9] Funds are allotted by formula grants to states (which in turn allocate funds to local entities) to provide training and related services to unemployed or underemployed individuals.

Services include job search assistance, skill assessment, career planning, case management, and training (including occupational skills training and on-the-job training). Training is conducted through a voucher system that allows individuals to attend training at eligible training providers (e.g., community colleges).

Employment Services under the Wagner-Peyser Act of 1933

The Wagner-Peyser Act established the Employment Service (ES) as a system jointly operated by DOL and the state employment security agencies. The central mission of the ES is to facilitate the match between individuals seeking employment and employers seeking workers. ES funds are allotted from DOL to the states through a formula grant. Typically, UI recipients

[9] The workforce development system designed by WIOA is premised on universal access, such that an adult age 18 or older does not need to meet any qualifying characteristics in order to receive core services. However, Section 134(c) of WIOA stipulates that priority is to be given to recipients of public assistance and other low-income individuals. It is left to the discretion of the local Workforce Development Board, in consultation with the state's governor, to determine how this prioritization is implemented.

must register with the ES. Jobseekers who are not eligible for UI may also register with the ES.

ES offers an array of services to job seekers and employers, including career counseling, job search workshops, labor market information, job listings, applicant screening, and referrals to job openings. States provide ES services through three tiers of service delivery: self-service, facilitated self-help, and staff-assisted. As the names of the tiers imply, progressively more active staff involvement is required as services range from internet job postings to career counseling.

Upon the establishment of the Unemployment Compensation (UC) program in 1935, ES offices also began to administer the UC "work test" requirements. These offices monitor UC claimants to ensure that they are able to work, available for work, and actively seeking work. For the recently unemployed, the ES processes UC income support claims while helping the individual find new employment.

Adult Education[10]

Education activities under the Adult Education and Family Literacy Act (AEFLA) are a mandatory AJC partner.[11] AEFLA provides formula grants to states to fund basic educational services at the high school level and below, as well as English language courses. States typically subgrant federal funds to local providers (such as school districts or community colleges) that provide the actual classes.

Programs Targeted by Circumstances of Job Loss

The programs discussed in this section are available to workers who are involuntarily separated from their jobs and meet other criteria. In some

[10] For more information on Adult Education and AEFLA, see CRS Report R43789, *Adult Education and Family Literacy Act: Major Statutory Provisions*, by Benjamin Collins.

[11] AEFLA was created by Title II of WIA and reauthorized as Title II of WIOA. As such, adult education programs may also be referred to as "Title II" programs.

cases, workers who have been notified of a layoff but have not yet been separated from their jobs may also be eligible for these programs.

Dislocated Worker Employment and Training Activities

This program provides formula grants to states to provide services to dislocated workers. To qualify as a dislocated worker, an individual must have been laid off from employment, sufficiently attached to the workforce (e.g., eligible for unemployment benefits), and unlikely to return to the occupation or industry from which the worker was laid off. Services available under the Dislocated Worker program include job search assistance, skill assessment, career planning, case management, and training (including occupational skills training and on-the-job training).

Approximately 80% of Dislocated Worker funds are allotted by formula grants to states (which in turn allocate funds to local entities) to provide training and related services to qualified unemployed individuals. The remainder of the appropriation is reserved by DOL for National Dislocated Worker Grants, which, in part, provide funds to states or entities that are affected by major economic dislocations, such as plant closures or mass layoffs.

Trade Adjustment Assistance (TAA) Program for Workers Adversely Affected by Foreign Trade[12]

Workers whose job loss is attributable to outsourcing or increased imports may be eligible for the TAA program. To be eligible for TAA benefits, a group of workers must petition DOL to certify that foreign trade "contributed importantly" to their job loss. Once a group is certified, individual workers may receive benefits through the AJC system. TAA provides reemployment services, training subsidies, and income support while in training. TAA-certified workers age 50 and over who pursue reemployment at a lower wage may participate in a wage insurance program.

[12] For more information on TAA, see CRS Report R42012, *Trade Adjustment Assistance for Workers*, by Benjamin Collins.

Programs Targeted by Jobseeker Characteristics

The programs discussed in this section determine eligibility by workers' personal characteristics. These eligibility requirements may or may not include economic characteristics such as individual or household income.

Vocational Rehabilitation (VR) for Workers with Disabilities[13]

State VR agencies provide employment-related services to individuals with disabilities. These agencies are funded by a combination of federal formula grants and state funds.[14] To be eligible for VR services, an applicant must establish that (1) he or she has a physical or mental impairment that results in a barrier to employment and (2) that the applicant would benefit from VR services. VR services are customized to each client and may vary. Services include (but are not limited to) counseling, job search assistance, training, and support services in the workplace.

Job Corps[15]

This primarily residential job training program provides a range of services to low-income individuals between the ages of 16 and 24. The purpose of the Job Corps program is to provide disadvantaged youth with the skills needed to obtain and hold a job, enter the Armed Forces, or enroll in advanced training or higher education. In addition to receiving academic and employment training, youth also engage in social and other services to promote their overall wellbeing. Services include educational support, work-based learning, counseling, and other support services.

---

[13] The VR state grants program is administered by the Department of Education. For more information on the VR state grants program, see CRS Report R43855, *Rehabilitation Act: Vocational Rehabilitation State Grants*, by Benjamin Collins.

[14] States must match their federal VR grants so that the federal share of VR funding is no more than 78.7%.

[15] For more information on youth programs, including Job Corps and WIA Youth, see CRS Report R40929, *Vulnerable Youth: Employment and Job Training Programs*, by Adrienne L. Fernandes-Alcantara.

Currently, there are 125 Job Corps centers in 48 states, the District of Columbia, and Puerto Rico.[16]

Youth Activities

This WIOA-authorized state formula grant program provides funding for training and related services to certain youth who are in school or out of school. A youth is eligible for services funded by this program if the individual is between the ages of 14 and 21 (or 24 for out-of-school youth) and meets other statutory criteria regarding income (primarily for in-school youth only) and/or barriers to employment.

Eligible participants in a program funded by these grants receive services that provide assistance in achieving academic and employment success through activities that improve educational and skill competencies and foster effective connections to employers. Such services include those involving educational achievement, employment services, linkages between educational achievement and employment, and additional support services.

Community Service Employment for Older Americans (CSEOA) Program[17]

CSEOA (Title V of the Older Americans Act) is a formula grant program, also known as the Senior Community Service Employment Program (SCSEP), which provides funding to promote part-time employment opportunities for unemployed low-income individuals who are age 55 or older. In addition to the age and income requirements to participate, individuals must generally have limited prospects of securing unsubsidized employment. The CSEOA provides funding to states and national sponsor organizations for subsidized employment in a variety of community-service activities, such as working at community centers, libraries, or schools. Participants in the program may receive training,

---

[16] Centers are in every state except New Hampshire and Wyoming. The DOL FY2016 budget justification states that centers in these two states are scheduled to open in program year 2015. See http://www.dol.gov/dol/budget/2016/PDF/ CBJ-2016-V1-05.pdf.

[17] For more information on CSEOA programs, see CRS Report RL33880, *Funding for the Older Americans Act and Other Aging Services Programs*, by Angela Napili and Kirsten J. Colello.

counseling, transportation, and placement assistance into unsubsidized employment.

Jobs for Veterans State Grants (JVSG) Program[18]

JVSG provides grants to states to fund state personnel positions that provide employment services to and on behalf of veterans. JVSG-funded personnel are divided into Disabled Veteran Outreach Program (DVOP) personnel and Local Veterans' Employment Representative (LVER) personnel. DVOP personnel provide direct employment services to disabled and other high-need veterans. LVER personnel perform outreach to local employers, conduct employment workshops for veterans, and work with other AJC personnel to provide employment-related services to veterans.

JVSG does not provide funding for training, though DVOP and LVER personnel may refer veteran jobseekers to programs administered by the Department of Veterans Affairs that provide funding for education and training. Veterans also receive priority of service in all DOL administered employment and training programs for which they qualify.[19]

Other AJC Partner Programs

In addition to the formula grant programs discussed in prior sections, WIOA also identifies several competitive grants and other programs as mandatory AJC partners. These programs differ from the formula grants discussed previously either because they are not widely available (in the case of competitive grants) or because they provide support to educational or community entities rather than directly to individuals (in the case of the programs discussed under the "Other Mandatory Partner Programs" heading).

---

[18] JVSG and other employment-related programs for veterans are discussed in CRS Report R42790, *Employment for Veterans: Trends and Programs*, coordinated by Benjamin Collins.

[19] Priority of service for veterans was established by the Jobs for Veterans Act (P.L. 107-288). The priority of service provisions are in statute at 38 U.S.C. 4215 and clarified in regulations at 20 C.F.R. 1010.

YouthBuild Program[20]

Authorized by Section 171 of WIOA, this competitive grant program funds projects that provide education and construction skills training for disadvantaged youth. Participating youth gain work experience, job training, education (a GED or preparation for secondary education), and leadership development by working to rehabilitate and construct housing for homeless and low-income families.

Native American Program

Authorized by Section 166 of WIOA, this competitive grant program provides training and related services to low-income Indians, Alaska Natives, and Native Hawaiians through grants to Indian tribes and reservations and other Native American groups.

Migrant and Seasonal Farmworker Programs

Authorized by Section 167 of WIOA, this competitive grant program provides training and related services, including technical assistance, to disadvantaged migrant and seasonal farmworkers and their dependents through discretionary grants awarded to public, private, and nonprofit organizations.

Other Mandatory Partner Programs

Community Services Block Grants (CSBGs) provide federal funds to states, territories, and tribes for distribution to local agencies to support a wide range of community-based activities to reduce poverty.[21] WIOA specifies that employment and training activities carried out with CSBG funds must partner with AJCs. CSBG is administered by the Department of Health and Human Services.

The Perkins Act provides funds to states to support vocational and technical career programs at secondary and postsecondary institutions.

---

[20] At the time of the enactment of WIA, YouthBuild was administered by the Department of Housing and Urban Development. The program was moved to DOL and authorization was added to WIA in 2007 by the YouthBuild Transfer Act (P.L. 109-281).

[21] For more information on CSBG, see CRS Report RL32872, *Community Services Block Grants (CSBG): Background and Funding*, by Karen Spar.

Postsecondary activities supported under this act are a mandatory AJC partner.[22] All Perkins programs are administered by the Department of Education.

Table 3. Employment and Training Programs Available to Unemployed Workers through the American Job Center Network

Program	Description	FY2015 Funding (in millions)
Employment and Training Programs Available to All Jobseekers		
Adult Employment and Training Activities	Provides job search assistance and training (including occupational skills training and on-the-job training). Training is conducted through a voucher system that allows individuals to attend training at eligible training providers.	$777
Employment Services under the Wagner-Peyser Act	Provides non-training services to job seekers and employers, including career counseling, job search workshops, labor market information, job listings, applicant screening, and referrals to job openings.	$664a
Basic Education under the Adult Education and Family Literacy Act	Provides educational services at the secondary level and below as well as English language training.	$583
Programs Targeted by Circumstances of Job Loss		
Dislocated Worker Employment and Training Activities	Provides employment services and training subsidies to workers who have involuntarily lost their jobs and demonstrated a specified level of labor force attachment.	$1,236[b]
Trade Adjustment Assistance Reemployment Services	Provides reemployment services, training services, and other benefits to workers whose job loss was attributable to international trade.	$659[c]

[22] For more information on programs authorized by the Perkins Act, see CRS Report R42863, *Carl D. Perkins Career and Technical Education Act of 2006: Background and Performance*, by Cassandria Dortch.

Table 3. (Continued)

Program	**Description**	**FY2015 Funding (in millions)**
Programs Targeted by Jobseekers Characteristics		
Vocational Rehabilitation	Provides customized counseling, training benefits, and other employment-related services to individuals with disabilities.	\$3,091[d]
Job Corps	Through primarily residential programs, provides disadvantaged youth with the skills needed to obtain and hold a job, enter the Armed Forces, or enroll in advanced training or higher education.	\$1,688
Youth Activities	Provides funding for training and related services to certain youth who are in school or out of school. A youth is eligible for services funded by this program if the individual is between the ages of 14 and 21 (or 24 for out-of-school youth) and meets other statutory criteria.	\$832
Community Service Employment for Older Americans (Title V of Older Americans Act)	Provides funding for subsidized employment in a variety of community-service jobs. To be eligible, a participant must be unemployed, age 55 or over, and demonstrate limited potential to enter unsubsidized employment.	\$434
Jobs for Veterans State Grants	Provides state personnel positions that provide employment-related services to veterans and outreach to local employers.	\$175
Competitive Grants and Other Programs		
Migrant and Seasonal Farmworkers Program	Provides training and related services to disadvantaged migrant and seasonal farmworkers and their dependents.	\$82
YouthBuild	Provides education and construction skills training for disadvantaged youth by rehabilitating and constructing housing for homeless and low-income families.	\$80
Native American Programs	Provides training and related services to low-income Indians, Alaska Natives, and Native Hawaiians.	\$46

Source: Department of Labor FY2015 operating plan at http://www.doleta.gov/grants/find_grants.cfm and Department of Education FY2015 Congressional Action Budget Summary at http://www2.ed.gov/about/overview/ budget/budget15/15action.pdf.

Note: Partner programs that do not primarily provide employment and training services to individuals are excluded from this table.

[a] Funding level is limited to funding for grants to states.

[b] Includes National Dislocated Worker Grants set-aside.

[c] Funding level reflects FY2015 funding for all TAA for workers activities. TAA is mandatory spending and may be subject to sequestration. Funding level in the table is post-sequestration funding for FY2015. Original appropriation was $710 million.

[d] VR state grants are mandatory spending and may be subject to sequestration. Funding level in the table is post-sequestration funding for FY2015. Original appropriation was $3.3 billion.

INDEX

E

F

L

M

N

O

P

Q

R

S

T

U

V

W

Y

Small Business Considerations, Economics and Research. Volume 9

Editors: Peter R. Bennett and Margaret O. Myers

Series: Business Issues, Competition and Entrepreneurship

Book Description: This book is a compilation of CRS reports on the Small Business Administration's (SBA's) Small Business Investment Company (SBIC). The opening report discusses the program's statistics, structure and operations.

Hardcover ISBN: 978-1-53614-353-9
Retail Price: $150

Information, Communication, and Automation Ethics in the Knowledge Society Age

Editor: Spyros G. Tzafestas (National Technical University of Athens, Athens, Greece)

Series: Ethical Issues in the 21st Century

Book Description: Information, communication and automation technology (ICAT) ethics is the branch of applied ethics and technoethics which investigates the social and ethical issues of the integrated multidisciplinary ICAT field in the broad sense that includes all kinds of automated systems through the use of ICT and computer based systems.

Hardcover ISBN: 978-1-53614-391-1
Retail Price: $230

Understanding Six Sigma: Concepts, Applications and Challenges

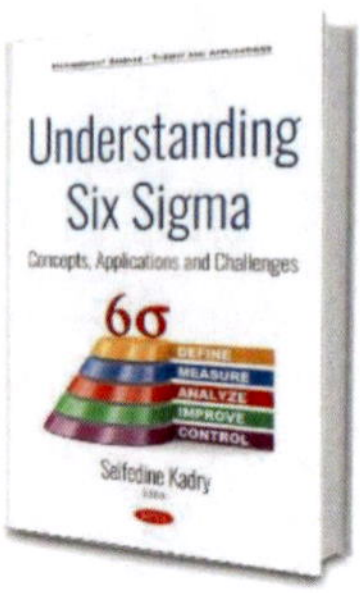

Editor: Seifedine Kadry (Beirut Arab University, Beirut, Lebanon)

Series: Management Science – Theory and Applications

Book Description: *Understanding Six Sigma: Concepts, Applications and Challenges* includes seven excellent chapters that have been prepared using state-of-the-art methodologies by professional researchers in this domain from seven different countries.

Softcover ISBN: 978-1-53614-174-0
Retail Price: $95

Unemployment: Economic, Political and Social Aspects

Editor: Tabitha Fletcher

Series: Economic Issues, Problems and Perspectives

Book Description: This book discusses unemployment and its relations to economic, political and social aspects. The first chapter studies the relationship of unemployment to the level of confidence that characterizes some macroeconomic relevant agents, such as consumers or investors.

Hardcover ISBN: 978-1-63485-181-7
Retail Price: $190